UNBROKEN BOY

UNBROKEN BOY

a memoir of hope and survival

Elisio Depina

Library of Congress Control Number:		2015909744
ISBN:	Hardcover	978-1-5035-7889-0
	Softcover	978-1-5035-7890-6
	eBook	978-1-5035-7891-3

Print information available on the last page

Rev. date: 06/17/2015

To order additional copies of this book, contact:
Xlibris
1-888-795-4274
www.Xlibris.com
Orders@Xlibris.com
709439

Dedication

I dedicate this book to all humans as evidence that we have the potential, power, courage, and strength within us to overcome any obstacles. All we have to do is acknowledge these gifts and implement them in any given situation without losing hope. No matter how bad the circumstance is, we must never, and I mean *never* even think about giving up.

ABOUT THE AUTHOR

I recently graduated from the University of New Haven with a master's degree in public administration. However, I chose to work in the field of counseling instead because I want to ensure no one lives a life like I experienced. Presently, I work as a young adult counselor at the Work Place, a nonprofit career center assisting students to prepare for the Massachusetts Comprehensive Assessment System (MCAS). I also help young adults find employment and connect them to community resources, such as shelter and GED programs. Using my personal story, I motivate and advise students to continue their education. When I am not working or writing, I am a motivational speaker to middle school, high school, and college students.

FOREWORD

I Hate Electric Cords . . .

CHAPTER 1

Life with Grandmother

I don't know if it happened by coincidence or if I was fated for a life of constant challenges. Did the choices I made as a five-year-old set me on the path I am on today? If so, what forces influenced those choices . . . ?

I was born on Friday, October 2, 1987, in São Jorge, on Fogo Island in Cape Verde. Cape Verde, located about 350 miles off the coast of Western Africa, means "green place" because of its lush vegetation during the rainy season. It is divided into ten islands, each surrounded by the Atlantic Ocean. On Fogo, most people raised animals and cultivated the land for a living. Fogo's economy never really had a chance to develop because of the lack of rain and the fact that only four of the ten islands had fertile soil. Indeed, one of them, Santa Luzia, was unpopulated. When I was growing up, there were only two socioeconomic levels on Fogo—poor and wealthy as the government devoted most of its attention and resources to the wealthy.

Since the poor didn't have a viable source of income, they worked the fields, digging the holes to plant seeds and then nurturing the crops through the harvest. Some people would plant just enough for personal use while others would sell their crops. Fogo, indeed, was the largest producing island of agricultural commodities, such as corn, vegetables, meat, and milk. It actually provided goods for the eight populated islands.

When I was born, my father, David, was twenty seven years old, and was trim and agile with dark skin and dark curly hair. He loved fishing and spent the majority of his weekends involved in that pastime. He also loved to cook. Before he immigrated to the United States, he was the best male chef in São Jorge. He was also well-known because he owned a small tractor, and he would volunteer to help people work on their projects.

My mother, Noemia, known as Nena, had long black hair that fell to her hips. She had light skin and stood just over five feet tall. Nena, who couldn't say no, would feed everyone from her neighborhood, even if it meant going hungry herself.

A couple of months after my birth, my father left for the United States, leaving my twenty-year-old mother and me behind. Immigrating to the United States is the dream of most Cape Verdean because they—we—envision it as a land of opportunity. My father immigrated with the intent to petition a visa for my mother and me, but he changed his mind after people wrongly accused my mother of cheating on him during his absence.

After I was born, my maternal grandmother, Tania, came from Campana, also on Fogo, to São Jorge to see her new grandson. I totally won her over. Because my father was living in the United Stated, and my mother was very young, my grandmother believed it was more practical for her to raise me. My mother and grandmother debated over my custody, but Tania told my mother that she could visit any time in Campana, which was only five miles north of São Jorge. After a six-month battle, my grandmother finally convinced my mother and returned with me to Campana.

Grandmother's house was about one mile from the road, surrounded by only a few other houses, about five hundred yards apart. The little community consisted of only ten families. Thus, our neighbors had a close relationship among each other. In fact, they spent most of their time at my grandmother's house, where they would exchange food, water, and even clothing, while sharing the news of the day.

My grandmother was a loving person. She was excited that I would be living with her even though she had nine children of her own. Two were still living with her—sixteen-year-old Pedro and eighteen-year-old Miquel. According to my mother, I was an adorable baby, constantly smiling and laughing. My grandmother showed me more affection than she did to her own children and took me everywhere with her. Pedro and Miquel were jealous because I was the first in the family to be read bedtime stories.

My grandmother always found a way to make me laugh. I loved it when she would throw me up in the air and catch me. Also, I was fascinated at how easily she could remove my nose and then reattach it. She would cross her fingers, make a nose shape, place them over my nose, and then quickly remove them, pretending she had my nose in her hands.

As well as playing with me, my grandmother would buy me toys. When I was two, she bought me little cars and motorcycles, and as I grew older, she replaced them with soccer balls, a little piano, and bigger cars. I was the only child in my neighborhood to own toys. As a result, I became the most popular kid in the small community, and everyone would come to play with me.

When I turned four, I attended the local kindergarten. Early in the morning, my grandmother would wake me up, help me get dressed, feed me breakfast, and walk me to school, which was a small building, about a mile down the road from our house. In the afternoon, she would pick me up, and whenever I refused to walk, she would give me a piggyback ride home. Once at home, she would prepare me lunch and give me snacks that she had hidden for me. Our friendship grew stronger every second. Miquel and Pedro would sometimes complain about how attached my Tania and I had become.

Even though Uncle Miquel was eighteen years old and my mother's closest brother, he was a little jealous of the relationship between my grandmother and me. However, he still loved me and would build me toy cars from wood and tin cans and often played with me. One day, he built a huge wooden car for me to ride in. He pushed and pulled me in that car everywhere in the neighborhood.

Miquel also helped me fly kites, the most popular activity in Campana. Everyone would build kites and then go up on a high hill and fly them in the gusty Cape Verde winds. Miquel would make five or six large kites a day for me, knowing that I would break one every half hour. Because a kite could easily pull me away, Miquel would tie one end of a soft rope onto my foot and the other end onto his foot. Every time he felt a strong wind, he would immediately grab both my feet, preventing the gust from whisking me away.

In 1990, Grandmother Tania began suffering from sharp pain, which continued for almost two years. Because Cape Verde was an undeveloped country, modern medical technology was unavailable, so the doctors were unable to diagnose her correctly. Every time she went to see them, they told her it was impossible to treat her because they couldn't figure out her disease.

Through her pain, she remained a strong person, and even when she was suffering back and chest pains and constant headaches, she always had a smile on her face. She never neglected me or shared her pain with me. Instead, she showed me unconditional love around the clock.

My grandmother loved to give, taking care of others but often neglecting herself. My loving grandmother passed away in 1992, leaving a little boy without his best friend.

CHAPTER 2

Farm Life: Too Much, Too Young

After my grandmother's death, my mother was living on the island of Praia. She was struggling to survive on her own and couldn't afford to support me. So she asked my uncle Joao to temporarily take custody of me while she straightened out her life. Uncle Joao lived in Ponta Verde, about twenty minutes from Campana and about fifteen minutes from São Jorge. Although he wasn't available to take care of me because he also spent most of his time on Praia, he agreed to leave me with his wife, Mary, and her mother, Catia. Thus in 1993, at the age of five, I moved to Ponta Verde.

"Where are we going?" I asked Uncle Joao after exiting from a car.

He glanced at me and went to pay the carfare. He then handed me my little backpack and held my hand with his left and my suitcase in his right. We began marching.

"Where are you going?" I asked again after about ten minutes of walking.

"You are going to stay with Mary for a while," he uttered.

"Who is Mary?"

"She is my wife. You are going to have a lot of fun with her."

"How long am I going to stay with her?" I asked, breathing heavily.

"I don't know."

"Until my grandma comes from Praia?"

I stopped and looked up to make eye contact.

He dropped the suitcase.

From bended knee, he placed his hand under my chin and gently raised it until our eyes met. "Buddy, I don't know exactly when your grandma is coming, but she will be here soon."

"I miss Grandma." He hugged me tight.

"I know you do. We all do." There was a short pause.

"What about this? Why don't we go to Mary's so you can play with all your toys?" He teasingly poked me in the chest.

"Okay." I smiled. "I'm going to play with those cars my grandma gave me."

"There you go! Do you want to play a game?"

"Yes," I replied, unsure.

"Do you see that tree over there?" He pointed to a tree about two yards away. "Whoever gets there last carries the other person to the house."

"That's not fair! I can't carry you!" I looked at him in disbelief. "You are too heavy!"

"Then you must win!"

"Can you hold my backpack then?"

"Sure!"

"Can I have running start because you have longer legs?"

He shook his head, smiling. "Sure! Sure, I guess. I guess that's only fair."

"Okay. I will tell you when to start running." I ran about twenty feet. "Don't start running yet!" I yelled. I ran another thirty feet and yelled again, "Don't start running yet!" When I past the halfway mark, I yelled, "You can start running now!" I ran as fast as I could and won a free ride home.

Upon arrival, Mary was waiting on the front porch and wobbled down the stairs to help Uncle Joao with the suitcase. Uncle Joao lowered me to the ground.

"Oh my God, he looks just like his mother," Mary commented, excited. "What's your name?"

She bent her knees to level with my height. She switched a tobacco from one side of her mouth to the other.

"Clesio."

I turned my head sideways, avoiding the repugnant smell of tobacco.

"Catia is preparing lunch. Are you hungry?"

I shook my head as she led us to the kitchen.

Mary was in her early fifties and had a broken arm that had never properly healed, making it hang uselessly. She was a frightening looking woman. Her hair was black with white at her temples, and always sticking up at odd angles. Sometimes she would pull it back into a tight bun or cover it with a handkerchief if she didn't feel like washing it. Her black teeth glistened every time she opened her mouth, and saliva bubbled in the several places where her teeth were missing from years of chewing tobacco. Her lower lip always seemed to pull to the left, as if trying to hide the huge mole on the left side of her chin. She was mean and heartless. She would frown and raise her voice every time she spoke to me and every time she came near me, I always felt uncomfortable, so I always tried to avoid making eye contact with her threatening black eyes.

Catia was also afraid of her. Catia was a sweet-natured woman with fine white hair she usually kept covered with a handkerchief. Her teeth were also black and missing from chewing tobacco, but her kind brown eyes always tried to offer comfort. She was so nice that Mary took vicious advantage of her. Catia was in her seventies, so Mary ran the household. Neither Mary nor Catia were able to perform heavy tasks, so my moving in meant the world to them, and they were extremely excited.

As we got closer to the kitchen, I could see a cloud of smoke exiting through the kitchen door and holes on the walls. Inside of the kitchen was a pile of woods leaned against the left side of the wall. There were also dirty plates, utensils, and other appliances all over the kitchen floor.

Mary sat on a large round wood in the middle of the kitchen. She immediately grabbed a round bucket filled with brown colored water and began washing dishes. Joao sat on a piece of wood near the door to avoid the cloud of smoke, and I leaned against him.

"Mama, have you noticed how he looks just like his mother?" Mary asked with a subdued smile.

Catia paused adding woods to the fire and looked at me. "Oh yeah, you are right! He has all the resemblance of his mother."

"No, he has his father's nose. His father has a pointy nose just like his," Joao said, pointing at my nose.

"His father never came back since he left, right?" Mary asked Joao as if she already knew the answer.

"No. never."

"Do you miss your father?"

Mary reached for my arm with her wet hand, but I instantly snatched my arm away.

I shook my head. "I miss grandma!" I took a remote car out of my backpack. "My grandma gave this before she left for Praia," I said while holding the car in the air for them to see.

"You grandma is no—"

"Yes, grandma went to Praia for a few months," Joao quickly interrupted, nodding at Mary. There was uncomfortable silence. "Is the food almost ready because I have to get my stuff ready for Praia?"

"Yeah, it's ready. Are you still leaving tomorrow?" Catia asked Joao.

"No. Friday."

"Oh yeah, today is only Wednesday."

"Can go to Praia with you to see grandma?"

"No. You have to stay so you can register for school. But I will bring grandma to see you," he lamented.

"Okay."

After we ate, Joao left and Catia gave a quick tour of the house. Even at age five, I knew from that day I was going to experience the worst time of my life.

Mary and Catia's house was isolated from society, located about five miles away from the road, up a hill. The closest house to us was about a mile away. The house itself was frightening because it looked like a haunted house. A portion of its back wall looked as though it could collapse any time. The house appeared to be at least a hundred years old, and there was concrete crumbling from the walls. Half its interior floor was paved, but the other half was unfinished, covered with dirt. Its yard was surrounded by plain looking rock walls. Most of those rocks were falling off, leaving rubble scattered around the yard.

The kitchen was detached from the house and sat about a fifth of a mile away. It was a dilapidated little building, with walls of stones placed gingerly on top of each other, a dirt floor, and a wooden door that was off its hinges, but wedged in to keep it closed.

Inside the house, there was no electricity. That meant no technology of any kind. We didn't have television, radio or electric lights. At night we used crude lanterns made from soda cans, cloth, and petroleum.

The moment I stepped inside the house, I felt shadow in my heart, which at the time I couldn't figure out why. But with time, my feeling became clear. Just a couple of weeks after my arrival all my toys disappeared and every time I asked for them, no one knew their whereabouts. Similar to my toys, I could never get an honest answer about my grandma. But worse, even at age five, I was given the full responsibility to take care ten goats, two cows, twenty chickens, two donkeys, and five pigs.

One evening, only my second week at the house, Mary took me to our farm to train me on how to take care of animals. It was still humid outside, but there was fresh air breezing by time to time. Mirage could be seen in the distance, and as we approached the animals' shelters, I could hear goats, cows, and donkey crying.

"Do you hear them? They are all thirsty." May shook her head in disappointment. "You have to listen up very carefully because I don't have time to repeat myself. Normally, you have to carry water from home to give to the animals. But lucky for you, today I already paid someone to bring it here. Look here!" she bent and grabbed a yellow five-gallon battle. "I think you are strong enough to carry this. You just may have to do multiple trips. But you will get the hang of it. Once you bring the water, deposit it into the barrel over there," she explained, pointing to a black metal barrel under a tree between two cows and five goats. We walked closer to the barrel. I got on my tiptoes to look inside and it was more than a half way full.

"How am I supposed pour water into that if I can barely reach it?"

"That's no problem at all. Just go around, stand on top the wall there, and pour it in. You don't even have to make an effort. Do you understand?"

"Yeah."

"It's pretty simple." She glimpsed at me sideway. "See this water tap?" She pointed to a metal water tap attached near to the bottom of the barrel. "You place this water bucket under this water tap, turn it counterclockwise to fill the bucket and then turn it clockwise to stop." She grabbed a black bucket and showed me how to do it. "Got it?"

"Yeah," I said, unsure.

"It's pretty simple. Now it's your turn." She handed me another bucket. Hesitating, I knelt down, placed the bucket under the water tap, and I gathered my muscles. I tried but the water tap didn't move. I tried again but nothing happened. I tried this time, using both hands, and the water tap suddenly turned too wild, causing the water to splash all over me and the ground. Mary promptly pushed me away and turned it off. "After you give water to all the animals," she resumed explaining, "It's important to move any animal that's directly under the sun. You know, they have feelings too. See, that goat over there needs to be moved under a shadow." I looked at her, unclear what to do next. "What are you waiting for, go move it? There's a shadow under the tree over there." She nudged.

"All right!" I slowly stepped toward the goat. I looked at her, hoping for any direction, but she stood there, silent, with hands crossed over her chest. Uncertain, I quietly tiptoed behind the goat and untied it from the tree. Then I tried pulling it toward the shadow, but it didn't move an inch. I stared at Mary for assistance, but she remained speechless. I tried again. Nothing. I took a deep breath, gathered my courage, and inched in front of the goat. I grabbed the goat by its two horns and pulled it forward as hard as I could. Still no movement. "Come on!" I pledged, irritated. Before closing my mouth, the goat hit my stomach with its horns and threw me a few steps back. I felt the urge to cry but fought the pain. Embarrassed, I looked at Mary, and she was fighting not to laugh.

"Get up and try again." I could tell she was getting inpatient.

I grabbed the hope and wrapped it around my wrist to gain leverage. I tried again. The goat suddenly started running toward the opposite direction, causing me to fall to my stomach. While still down, it pulled my stomach against sharp rocks and pebbles for about seven feet before I could let it go free. The tear filled my eyes, but I fought the urge. The skin from my arms and belly peeled off.

I stood up and started walking home, but Mary promptly jumped in front of me. "Hey! Hey! You can't just quit because thing is tough or painful. Get back there. We still have to feed them, you know."

Without a word, I moved to the side, trying to go home regardless. She grabbed my shirt from behind, pulled me in front of her, and pushed against my chest as hard as she could.

I landed backward on top of a pile of rocks. I felt a sharp pain on my back, head, and butt. I could feel anger building inside of me. I felt the urgency for crying, but I clenched my teeth, refusing the tears. "Why? Why did you push me? I didn't even do anything wrong." But this time I just couldn't hold the tears any longer. I broke crying, still sitting down.

"There's no reason to cry. You are a big boy now." She crouched right next to me and wrapped her arm around my neck. She tried to hide her sparkly smile.

I instantly snatched her arm and pushed away as hard as I could. "Get your hand away from me!" I screamed in a high-pitched voice, while sliding away from her.

"Gosh. I was only trying to help." She got to her feet, shook her head, and went to tie the goat. Wincing with pain, I forced myself to my feet. "The last thing you need to do," she continued as if nothing had happened, "Is feeding the animals. Again, normally, you have to search for hay. But because today is your lucky day, it's already piled here. You just need to distribute them. Understand?"

I wiped the tears and opened my mouth to speak but nothing came out. I tried again. "Where do I search for hay?"

"Oh, that's the fun part. You just have to look for it until you find it. As you can see, people already collected all the hay around here, so you may have to walk far. The farther you go toward uncultivated fields, the more successful you will be."

After explaining, she went picking fruits, sat under a tree, and ate them, while I fed the animals.

Promptly after the training, Mary began waking me up every day at 4:00 a.m. to feed those animals. After taking care of the animals, I had to cut more hay to feed them in the afternoon. Then I had to carry those hay bales for two miles every day. It wasn't until 10:00 a.m. that I would have my first meal, which was a glass of water with sugar and two little cookies.

As I grew older, my responsibilities grew with me. By age seven, I was responsible not only for taking care of the animals but also for the whole agricultural process. Working on the farm was a year-round process;

when one project ended, another started, and then the cycles were repeated. Producing crops for over twenty acres totally depended upon the dry and rainy seasons. Fertilizing began in early April, and the fields were continuously tended through the harvest in December and January. The digging began in May and continued through June and into July so the earth would be ready for green season rains that began in August.

The dry season was from January to the beginning of August. In early April, I would prepare the fields for planting. I would remove all the dead plants from the last crop and fertilize the soil. A mixture of animals' leftover feed and their excrement made a perfect natural fertilizer.

Although I hated all the farm work, I hated fertilizing the most. Every time I was asked to fertilize the fields, my heart would drop. One time I hurt myself just, trying to avoid fertilizing for a day. But Mary forced me to gather the fertilizer and carry it to distribute across the fields despite my dislocated arm. Combining the leftovers and excrement with water would generate a strong odor as well as release nasty looking insects. Many times, when I carried fertilizer on top of my head, I would feel little insects crawling on my body.

One day, an insect bit under my eye, and I couldn't see with one eye for almost a month because it got too swollen. Another reason I hated fertilizing was, breathing the stench without a mask was life-threatening, because it involved a two-mile trip. As well as the danger of the path itself, the fertilizer was heavy and uncomfortable, so I often had to shift it around as I carried it on my head. The more shifting, the more the odor and insects would be released, suffocating me.

The next step after fertilizing was digging holes for planting seeds, such as corn, peanuts, and beans. To finish the digging before the rains came, I was ordered to work all day, from my first meal at 10:00 a.m. until dark. It didn't matter whether there was torrential rain or extreme wind or heat. I worked even when the temperature was above one hundred degrees. The heat not only would burn my skull but also gave me terrible headaches. Still I wasn't allowed to go home until there was no longer any light in which to work. When Mary didn't bring any food, I had to search for fruits, potatoes, and peanuts in the fields. After the holes had been readied, I would return to each hole, fill it with a couple of different seeds, and then close it up. The planting took about a month.

Once that task was completed, my battle with the weeds began. Weeds, already in the soil, developed and multiplied much faster than the plants. Thus, they had significant advantage over the cultivated plants and often depleted much needed resources. They needed little water to grow, and they were very heat resistant. Weeds were my biggest threat because they grew so strong, they could prevent the plants from developing. I had to yank the weeds twice to save the crops. And yes, after "winning" the battle, I had to carry those unwanted weeds to feed the animals. By the time I finished, it would be the dry season, and the harvest would be ready.

January, the beginning of dry season, was even harder than the green season because harvesting and carrying crops by hand was exhausting. All the crops had to be harvested and stored by end of the January. During this period, I also had to transport water and hay from approximately two and a half miles, in order to feed the animals and perform other tasks, such as husking, grinding, and storing corn.

In addition to our farm near the house, we had approximately fifty acres for agriculture about two miles away, but because there were many hills and cliffs, the distance felt even longer. The steep and windy path ran right along the side of a drop of about ninety feet. Transporting goods from the fields to our house was very difficult, and it was especially dangerous on windy days. I was sent most frequently to gather and bring back feed for the animals to the storage area near the house. On weekends, I was expected to bring hay back instead.

Transporting hay on a windy day was treacherous for two reasons. The wind in Cape Verde blows very strong, and when I was moving against it, I had to fight to prevent the wind from pushing me backward. Then when it stopped suddenly, the absence of force would cause me to fall forward. When the wind was at my back, it was so strong that it carried me away. No matter which direction the wind was blowing, it was always my enemy; therefore, every time I was sent to gather hay, I feared I wouldn't make it back. I still remember my very first time carrying hay. I almost felt off a cliff because I didn't know the vagaries of the wind. It pushed me toward the edge of one cliff, and just when I was about to fall off, I threw my hay instead. I watched it bounce down the side of the cliff, and each crash was like a blow to my own body. I knew I now had to go back to get another one, or I would receive a beating if I returned empty-handed. Watching it finally come to a stop, scattered over the cliff-side, I tried not to cry as I turned back to find another bale and try again.

It never got easier. After ten trips, my energy to fight the wind would diminish more and more. I would make an average of twelve trips each day and still be expected to tend to the animals yet again, but I sluggishly completed my tasks as I wished for bed.

Conveying goods to markets was another hard job. Since the narrow access road was about one and a half miles away, I had to carry the goods by hand. The fact that I didn't own shoes made it even harder because Cape Verde has an extremely hot climate, and the soil was very hot. The heavy weight of the goods would add pressure to my steps and even burn the arches of my feet. The path to the road was covered with sharp rocks and broken glass. I would try to avoid them, but some always caught me by surprise, piercing my foot. I would try to hop off as quickly as I could, but the weight of the goods made this impossible, and instead, I would only lose my balance and step on another sharp stone. One time I looked back to see a trail of blood behind me. I could feel the sand working its way deep inside my cut, and I worried that it would become infected. What if I lost my foot? I started to walk on my heels to avoid getting more sand inside, and by the end of the trip, walking was almost too painful to bear.

This same procedure was also how materials were brought to the house. Sometimes it would take as many as twenty trips. One time Mary decided to fix our porch (as though it would make any difference). It took three weeks to carry the materials, such as sand, cement, and rocks. And of course, I had to carry more water.

During the dry season, people would run out of water because only small storage tanks were available. These tanks would hold only 1,500 to 2,000 gallons of water, which wasn't enough to sustain our needs as well as the animals.' The houses' roof tops were designed with sharp slants and gutters all around to catch as much water as possible. Pipes would be installed from the gutters to the tanks so when it rained, the water would travel through these pipes into the tanks. Since the tanks could hold only a limited amount of water, I was responsible for providing it when we ran out, which was usually about midseason. The source where we bought our water was a good three miles away. I had to carry the water on top of my head in a large plastic container that held twenty gallons of water. Every day I had to obtain enough water not only for our use but also to feed the animals. Most of the time, I was sent to buy water in the evening, after working all morning.

One day after I came home from digging holes, Mary handed me the massive water bottle. Without even a chance to change my dirty, sweaty clothing, I turned around and headed out for the water. With my muscles aching from digging, that twenty-gallon bottle seemed twice as heavy. I had to rest several times on the way back, placing the bottle at my feet. After taking a few minutes to myself, I tried to lift the bottle back up. My muscles screamed and started to shake with fatigue, making the water slosh precariously. I squeezed my eyes shut against the spasms and tried to steady the bottle on the top of my head, and I tried to make my feet move. When I was finally home, I slowly put the bottle down on the ground, afraid that any attempt at movement would make it fall. Mary opened the door and looked at me expectantly.

"Well, what are you waiting for, you lazy fool? Bring it in!"

CHAPTER 3

Living with Mary:
A Fight for Survival

Although farm work was exhausting, I would rather have spent my time working there than being at home because at least I felt like I had freedom when working in the field. At home, Mary would be on top of me, constantly giving me orders and criticisms. Also, I was more likely to be abused at home than in the field. Mary would constantly beat me with an electric cord that she had found in São Filipe City. She brought the electric cord to show Catia how electricity would travel, and before I knew it, the cord became my biggest enemy.

In addition to the grueling farm duties, I was responsible for performing house chores, often cleaning on the weekend even after I returned from working in the fields. I had to clean the house, do laundry, and perform other tasks, such as grinding corn. Mary barely cooked during the day. Instead, she would wait until I came home from work and expect me to make our evening meal.

Despite the pain and frustration, cooking was my favorite task, and it wasn't because I was a young man who liked to eat. It's because cooking was the least physically exhausting of all my chores. Since we didn't own a stove, I had to cook with wood. Cooking without a stove was frustrating, because it was difficult to keep the fire alive. Add to the scene a pot that sat precariously on top of three rocks, and I was always in fear that things would spill. Lighting the fire was a complicated task, which sometimes would take twenty minutes to half an hour. And, in order to keep the fire alive, I had to keep adding wood while trying not to knock over the pot. Even with all my attention, the flames would still die. I had to constantly blow on it, my lungs sometimes burning from the effort and exertion. I found myself having to bring my mouth as close to the fire as possible so the air would fan the flame and spread it. Being so close to it, I ran the risk of sucking in the ash as I took in a deep breath, possibly singing my lungs and also causing hot ash to fly into my face and eyes. One time, I unconsciously brought my face too close, and the fire burned my eyelashes, face, and arms. Of course, I would get no sympathy from Mary, who was less concerned about my safety and was more worried about her meal and not making a mess.

One night, after the stew had been cooking for a while, the flames started to die down, so I put wood on the fire. I knelt down on the dirt floor to fan the flames and ignite the new wood I had just put on. Trying not to put my face too close this time, I steadied my hand on one of the rocks, forgetting they were already hot from the fire. Instantly, the pain shot through my hand and arm. I pushed back quickly, and the rock wobbled. Suddenly the pot tipped, and an even greater, white-hot pain engulfed me as the boiling stew splashed all over me. I cried out from the intense pain and stumbled from the kitchen.

Mary came running and froze at the sight of me, standing dripping wet and scalded. Her face contorted in fury. She stood outside the kitchen door, forcing me back into the kitchen.

"Porkaria! You ruined my dinner," she spat. She looked around her for something to hit me with and spied a stick. Snatching it up, she advanced on me, raising it above her head and smashing it down forcefully on my burned skin as she screamed, "You never pay attention to anything you do! I think you do these things on purpose to piss me off!"

Shaking, I tried to turn away, giving her my back, but she moved around, aiming for the burned skin.

"Look at me when I talk to you!" she snapped, while she shoveled my back against the wall.

"Please don't hit me. I didn't do it on purpose. It was an accident," I pleaded, shielding my face and trying to deflect her blows.

"An accident? Huh! Do you think this is a joke?" She got closer, spitting all over my face as she spoke. I breathed a strong smell of tobacco, which she was chewing and switching back and forth to the sides of her mouth. "Don't make me kill you because I have no problem killing you right here, right now!"

Flinching, I slightly moved my head to the left to avoid her spit and the foul tobacco smell. She grabbed my neck, lifted me up, and then threw me as hard as she could to the ground on top of the hot water that was left from the spilled dinner. The hot water, along with my burnt body, made it seem like the blood was boiling inside me. As I attempted to quickly get up and remove myself from the scene, Mary placed her right foot against my chest and pressed down.

"You have no idea who you are playing with!" she said, crunching her teeth.

The pain was progressively getting worse, and now I could barely feel my hands and back. I grabbed her foot with my both tiny hands, trying to push her away, but I wasn't strong enough, so I lay there, feeling as if her foot could go right through me.

In what seemed like an eternity was probably just a couple of minutes later, she finally moved her foot, and I immediately got up, removed my wet clothing, and ran outside for fresh air. Mary instantly ran after me, reached for my hand, and pulled me back toward the kitchen. "Where do you think you are going? Get back in there and do it again. And this time you won't have any, since you're just wasting it all on the ground!" I scrambled back into the kitchen, surveying the mess through tear-filled eyes, and started all over again.

****

Cooking and abuse weren't my only problems. Some days Mary would demand that the house be cleaned, and I would be forced to stay home after feeding the animals, instead of tending to the duties on the farm. Cleaning the old house was an impossible task because the walls were peeling, producing dust that covered everything. When I tried to clean, it made things worse. Half of the interior floor was unfinished—it was covered with dirt. When I swept, the dust would spread throughout the house, making it unhealthy to breathe. Wind easily blew more dust inside the house because it was located in the center of an unlandscaped and unpaved lot. Suffice it to say, the house required cleaning all the time. I would get mad because immediately after I finished cleaning, it would be dirty again. It was an endless cycle, and Mary was never happy with the result.

Another disadvantage about cleaning the house was that we didn't have the proper cleaning supplies. Brooms were made of plants. I would collect branches and tie them together. The problem was that those homemade brooms were too weak to catch the dirt on the unfinished floor and easily fell apart. After one use, the leaves would begin to detach from the broom, and the broom itself would make more mess.

Cleaning the exterior of the house was even more tiring than cleaning the interior. The wind would blow all the trash and other debris from our farm and others into our yard. Every morning, I would find bottles, plastic bags, hay, and other trash piled in our yard. Because my makeshift brooms were too weak to handle all the trash, I had to pick up everything with my bare hands, and, of course, I had no gloves of any kind. Then I had to carry the trash to fields almost half a mile away, and I had no choice but to breathe unsanitary air and the blowing dust. Many times, in fact, I would suffocate with the effort.

Just as we didn't own a stove, we didn't own a washing machine. I had to launder our clothing by hand. Since Mary had a broken arm and Catia was too old to do the laundry, it was left to me to wash the clothing for all three of us. Our "washing machine" was a concrete tub about three feet in diameter and four feet tall. It had a stopper in the center and two indentations to hold the end of a galvanized washboard. Our clothing would need to be washed three times a week because we were so exposed to dust and dirt. It took about six hours to launder our jeans, sweaters, T-shirts, jackets, blankets, and bed sheets. After hours of pressing and rubbing the items against the galvanized washboard, my hands would start to hurt, but I wasn't allowed to stop until I finished.

****

Needless to say, it was tiring and depressing to be at home. We were so isolated that we would rarely if ever see people, or if we did, it would be in passing, and far in the distance. It would be months before people deliberately coming to our house. Believe it or not, even Mary loved when people visited us—visitors provided golden moments.

One day, Mary was excited to see two people, walking toward our house.

"Clesio? Clesio? Come here quick," Mary called to me.

Oh no, what now.

"What?" I asked with hesitation.

"There are two people walking in this direction. Can you see them?"

"Yes, but I can't tell who they are. They are too far away."

"Quick, go on the roof and look." I ran to the rooftop. "Can you tell who they are from there?"

"No. . . not yet." I watched attentively as the two people got closer and closer. "Oh, I think it is my brother Nelson and my sister Neminha." My lips quickly stretched into a smile.

"Get down here now!" Mary yelled.

I could detect frustration in her voice. I came down, and we waited for their arrival.

"Hi," said Neminha when she and Nelson finally arrived.

"Hi," I said with excitement. "What are you guys doing here?"

"We came to visit you," she said as she hugged me. "We haven't seen you in four years. You are so big now!"

"Come in," Mary said, laughing evilly.

Neminha put her arm around my neck. Nelson looked at me and smiled.

"No, it's fine. We can sit out here. We aren't going to stay long," Neminha responded.

With her arm still wrapped around my neck, she sat on a concrete bench, and lifted me onto her lap. A few minutes later, Mary went inside looking for Catia.

"Can you come and spend the weekend with us, Clesio?" asked Neminha, smiling.

I looked at her excitedly, then at Nelson. It would be great to spend a few days away from the nightmare life I had with Mary.

"Of course!" I exclaimed.

Nelson's face lit up. "We will go play soccer and go to the Salina Beach in São Jorge together," said Nelson as Mary returned and sat between Nelson and me.

"What are you kids talking about?" she asked sarcastically.

"Clesio is going to spend the weekend with us," Nelson responded, hesitating.

Mary instantly got up.

"He can't go!" she yelled. "He has a doctor's appointment," she added matter-of-factly. Neminha's head dropped in disbelief and disappointment. Nelson scowled. His eyebrows pointed down, and he ground his teeth.

My eyes widened. "What appointment?" I asked, confused.

Mary reached out and tapped my shoulder, signaling me to keep quiet. My blood turned into ice in response to the deception. There was no appointment, and she knew it!

"The appointment to check your head, don't you remember?" Mary asked.

"Can he reschedule it?" asked Neminha, her voice and eyes pleading.

"No, he has rescheduled it many times." Mary smirked. "I'm sorry, kids."

Neminha got up and looked at me as tears poured down her face. And they were starting to well up in my eyes too.

"Come on, Nelson, we have to go," she demanded.

"Why?" Nelson asked. "Why so soon?"

"Let's go! Stop asking a million questions!" she yelled as she descended the porch stairs.

Nelson followed without even having a chance to say a proper goodbye. I stood on the porch, watching them with tear-filled eyes as they vanished in the distance.

Shortly after, Catia came from the kitchen with a basket filled with fruits. "Where are your brother and sister?" She turned her head around, looking for them.

"They left," I responded, tears welling in my eyes.

"Why?"

"Because Mary didn't allow me to go with them."

Catia walked to me and placed her arm awkwardly around my shoulders. She turned to Mary. "Why didn't you let him go?" she asked firmly.

Mary immediately stood up and walked toward us. My heart pounded rapidly as my legs started to shake. *Please don't hit us, please don't hit us.*

"You, shut up!" she yelled. "It's none of your business. I'm the one who decides." She then turned to me and slapped me hard on the face. "Next time when I say you have a doctor's appointment, you keep shut. Because of you, now they think I am a bad person." *At least they are thinking the right thing.*

Anticipating the beating, I went to the kitchen, trying to avoid it, but Mary followed me. I sat on a piece of wood, facing down.

"Look at me when I talk to you!" she yelled, as she grabbed a hot metal rod near the fire and began to jab me with it.

"Why are you poking with the hot metal? I didn't even do anything!" I snapped back at her, already angry for not going with my siblings.

"Shut up! You shut up!"

She continued poking with the hot metal as my skin tore off with every poke. Anguishing in pain, I tried not to cry, but tears flowed regardless. With every poke, my heart felt as if it was being torn apart little by little until there was none remaining. I could smell my skin burn. I unconsciously closed my hands into tight fists, while clenching my teeth, wincing over the tormenting pain.

Even though the burning was severe and excruciating, not going with my siblings hurt me more.

After relentlessly burning my arms, legs, and chest for about five minutes, she walked away with a grimace. As soon as she left, I broke down crying inconsolably, punching and kicking the wall out of frustration. It took me a while before noticing my bleeding hands while my toenail was ripped off from kicking the wall. Desperate, I pulled my hair and dropped to the ground, crying. *When is this abuse going to end? Am I going to survive from this abuse?* The more I looked at my burn marks, the more I cried.

Mary returned to the kitchen a moment later, looking angry and frightening.

"Stop crying!" she demanded. I tried to fight the urge, but I couldn't control myself, and the tears flowed. "Stop crying before I give you something to cry about. You know what? Get out of my face! Get out! Get out before I kill you! Go take care of the animals."

Mary pulled my arm and pushed me out the door. I sprawled on top of pile of woods. Clenching my teeth, I snatched a thick and long piece of wood and smashed it in front of her.

"You want to kill me? Then go ahead. Do it right now!" I yelled firmly. "This life isn't worth living anyw—" Before I could even close my mouth, she hit my face with a stick, knocking my front tooth out. I immediately ran to take care of the animals.

I hate this stupid life. I don't even know why I am alive. To live like a slave? My life would be much simpler without the evil Mary.

I wobbled to a pile of hay, which I had gathered earlier from the farm and stored near the animals. I picked a bench, stumbled toward the two goats, and threw it in front of them as hard as I could, scattering it all over.

"Here! At least you get to eat. Me. Me, not only I didn't get to eat all day or go with my brother and sister, but I have to put up with Mary's abuse!" I snarled at the goats as if they could understand me, while angrily kicking the hay. Scared of my yelling, the goats tried to run away. One, in fact, ran so quickly that it reached the end of the rope that was holding it back, causing it to fall down. I looked into the animal's frightened eyes, and my head dropped. *Nice going, Clesio. They don't deserve that.* I walked to it, knelt down, and hugged it. "I'm sorry. It's not your fault. It's the evil's fault. I'm so frustrated with my life. But that isn't a reason for me to make your life miserable, too. I'm sorry." I wiped my tears. The other goat slowly inched to me. I wrapped my arm around its neck, still hugging the other one.

After I finished feeding the animals, I rushed inside, hoping to finally have dinner. Walking up the front stairs, I saw Mary and Catia carrying our dinner from the kitchen to the living room.

"What took you so long?" Mary paused and asked. *Oh crap, not again.*

"The donkey's leash was damaged, so I had to replace it," I lied. She continued walking to the living room without another word. I followed her.

"Go take a shower and go to bed!" Mary demanded.

"But—"

"But nothing," she interrupted. "Go take a shower this instant, or do you want more of what happened earlier?"

"When is the last time the kid ate something?" Catia confronted her. "Early this morning, right? It's now about eight o'clock at night. Don't you think he should eat something?"

"He has to learn his lesson. When I say no, I mean no. He embarrassed me in front of his brother and sister." She turned and took a step toward Catia. "He," she continued, "made me look like evil. He couldn't simply agree about his doctor's appointment."

"Does he have an appointment?"

"No, but that isn't the point. And you have to learn how to stay out of this. I'm responsible to raise him. I'm teaching him how to be disciplined! I'm teaching him manners. The boy has no manners!" Mary said, pointing at me.

"I am going to stay out of your way, but know when the boy collapses, you have to explain it to his mother. The only thing he ate was a piece of bread and a glass of water with sugar since 10:00 a.m."

Mary's face turned red. She frowned at me.

I took a step back.

"I'm not going to repeat myself again. Now get lost before I lose my temper."

I shook my head and slowly walked off to bed, without having taken a shower. My stomach growled the entire night.

****

My sleep was interrupted several times virtually every night. Mary would wake me every night to retrieve her belongings that she had forgotten in the kitchen, which was detached from the house, about two minutes away. It would be pitch-dark, and I used to be scared to death to walk in the dark by myself.

One night, Mary woke me up at 2:00 a.m. because she wanted to smoke her pipe, which was in the kitchen. It was raining and windy; worst of all, there was thunder and lightning—I was traumatized by thunderstorms and lightning. Growing up, Catia told me a story about how lightning struck several of her friends, killing them instantly. As a result of the story, such storms scared me to death. Every time I heard thunder, my heart would instantly stop. In fact, just hearing people talk about a possible thunderstorm would make my heart skip a beat. But Mary didn't care.

"Clesio? Clesio? Clesio?" Mary called while shaking me awake.

Mary and Catia slept together on a bed parallel to mine in the same room.

"What happened?" I mumbled.

My heart began to palpitate as I sat on the bed, trying to figure out what was going on. Mary reached my shoulder and shook me again.

"Get up and go get my pipe in the kitchen," she demanded.

"The poor kid is still sleeping. Can't you wait until morning?" Catia suggested in a fearful voice.

Mary's eyes widened in disbelief that Catia was interfering with her request.

"You shut up! Really? Now he is a poor kid!" Mary snapped at Catia.

Mary then walked to the bedroom door and opened it.

"You're still here? Get up already and go!" Mary yelled, pointing to the door.

She didn't care how scared I might be; she wanted her pipe. I felt fear building in my body. Everything began to shake as I heard the thunderstorm and saw lightning flashing in front of the door. *God, please save me and don't let lightning strike me.* As Mary demanded I go outside in the terrifying weather, I wondered how I was going to survive this one.

Nevertheless, I gathered my courage and went retrieving her pipe.

The rain instantly soaked my already baggy pants, and I tried to hold them up while running awkwardly around the water tank. A cat startled me as it darted across my path, making me skid on the mud, and my pant leg wrapped around the bottom of my foot, almost causing me to fall. Once I reached the kitchen door, I had to let my pants go so I could pick up the door with both hands and struggle to move it aside. I peered into the dark room, trying to force my eyes to see the outlines of the things inside, but they wouldn't work. Grabbing my pants in a tight fist and hauling them up to my waist, I reached out my other hand in front of me, expecting to touch the big cast-iron pot, crusty with soot. Trying to imagine the layout of the room from memory, I tried to think of where her stupid pipe might be. I moved to the left, feeling my way around the wall to where the table and the storage shelf would be. Her pipe had to be there.

I found the table and moved my hand slowly along the surface, but the pipe wasn't there. I turned suddenly, and a sharp pain cracked me in the forehead, causing me to stumble backwards a step. I shook my head slightly and reached up to find the storage shelf. I patted the surface, my hand feeling leftover food from that night's dinner and the empty cup she usually kept water in, but no pipe. She might have had it somewhere in the bedroom. I returned to the bedroom.

"I can't find it," I said very softy.

Mary immediately stood up abruptly, grabbed me by the neck, and viciously shoved me against the wall. I could feel my heart beating faster and faster as she frowned and glared into my eyes. I felt a cold breeze around my neck. The blood in my body turned into ice. I felt like crying, but I fought back the tears because I knew it would only worsen things.

She clenched her teeth. "You are useless," she said, slowly releasing my neck. "Go back there and find my pipe. And you better not come back until you find it if you don't want me to smash your head against the wall."

As I was walking out of the door, lightning flashed, and I instantly jumped back. Mary placed her two hands on my back and shoved me out as hard as she could.

"It isn't going to kill you!" she shouted at me.

But that's not what I was thinking. I landed on my arms on top of a pile of bricks, hitting and cutting my head in the process. I managed to get up, wincing from the pain in my head and arms. I gingerly touched the back of my head, my fingers feeling the warm, sticky blood. I started to panic. Then I began to comfort myself, *don't panic, don't panic. You will be okay.* Terrified, I hobbled back to the kitchen and continued to look for the elusive pipe. I became more and more worried because I realized I was losing a great deal of blood from the injury on my head and arm. I was confused and scared because I didn't know what to do. Should I return without the pipe? Should I continue the search? What if I don't find it on time? I couldn't return without the pipe, but if I didn't stop rummaging soon enough, I was going to bleed to death. Unaware of my bloody hands, from periodically checking the back of my head, I rubbed my face. Now I had blood in my eyes, mouth, and all over my face.

After forty minutes, I became more concerned about losing blood than having my head smashed against the wall, so I decided to go back without the pipe.

"Your pipe isn't there," I said crying.

Mary abruptly grabbed me by my collar, made a fist, and then swung it back. I flinched, closed my eyes, and waited for the punch. Right when she was about to punch my face, Catia interrupted her.

"Have you checked your pocket?" Catia yelled.

While still holding my shirt, she opened her fist and checked her pocket. There was the mysterious pipe.

"You are lucky," Mary stated, smiling as though everything was all right now.

Then I was ordered to go back to bed without any medical care. I watched Mary walk to her bed, sit down, and carefully fill and light her pipe. She inhaled deeply and sighed out a moment later, smoke twisting lazily through the air around her.

The back of my head throbbed painfully, but more than that was the hurt that she hadn't even apologized.

Two hours later, without having had any sleep and throbbing with pain, I rose to take care of the animals. I walked out the door, the wind now calm but the cold rain still pouring down on me.

CHAPTER 4

The Dark Side of Getting an Education

Ponta Verde had only one school system, which operated Monday through Friday, from 8:30 a.m. until 6:00 p.m., October through May. To accommodate all the students, there were two sessions—8:30 a.m. to 12:30 p.m. or 1:00 p.m. to 6:00 p.m.—and I attended the second session. The distance from the school to our house was about an hour's walk. But Mary demanded I arrive home no later than thirty minutes after school dismissal because I had to feed the animals and finish all the other chores before dark. If I was even a minute late, she would beat me with the abominable electric cord. To avoid beating, immediately after class, I would tear home. I never had time to socialize with friends. My friends would ask me why I always had to run home. Fearful that Mary would find out, I didn't answer them honestly. One day, however, I got distracted on my way home, and I lost track of time.

"Guys, check it out, a crazy woman is gaiting this way with a cord," one of my friends alarmed us. From the far distance, I couldn't identify the person; I could only tell that she was swaggering barefoot, with a piece of red clothing wrapped around her head. Her spiky hair was pointing outward. Suddenly, she crossed the street, positioning herself on the same side of the street as us. Curiously, we all stopped and watched the woman getting closer and closer.

"Is that Mary?" my neighbor Antonio asked with a worried look.

I stretched my eyes, hoping Antonio was wrong. "I hope not."

"Dude, that's definitely her. Look at her hair pointing out. She is the only one with the hairstyle."

"Shut up, Antonio! You are not helping."

I suddenly noticed my hands shaking. I froze looking at Mary swinging her arms back and forth, holding the cord firmly with her right hand. I felt sweat pouring down my body, and my legs felt heavy. I couldn't move.

Without hesitation, Mary advanced on me and began striking my body with the electric cord while my friends watched. Everyone was confused, terrified, and worried, and they stood silently as fear consumed them.

"When I tell you to be home by 6:30 p.m., I want you at home by 6:29 p.m. March home right now and go feed those poor animals!" she raged, still hitting me.

With my head down, attempting to avoid making eye contact with my friends, I rambled in front of her while she continually whipped me, all the way home. I could feel warm blood rolling down on my back.

Even after all the abuse and grueling labor, Mary was too cheap or maybe too coldhearted to buy me my immediate needs. I was never prepared for school because Mary, who didn't like to spend money, refused to provide me with school supplies. Thus, I didn't have a notebook, a pencil, or a pen. Many times, I had to use a brown paper bag as a notebook and burnt wood as a writing tool. I would cut pieces of paper from bags that held cement, punch holes in them, and then tie them together to make a notebook.

Nor did I have shoes or a backpack. I would attend school barefoot while carrying a plastic bag. My clothing was old and sometimes ripped.

I struggled to fit into my school environment. Since I was growing up mostly isolated from people, I had difficulty bonding with other students. I lacked social skills, so I preferred solitude. During the recess between classes, I would sit alone and try to rest. Since I could never rest at home, school was my only opportunity to take a break. However, students wouldn't leave me alone; they would bother me and make fun of my clothing and my school supplies. I became a target for bullying because I didn't fight back. For one thing, after working all day in the fields, I was too exhausted to fight. Also, Mary would beat me if she learned I was involved in a fight, even when it wasn't my fault. In addition, because my clothing was already old and ripped, it could easily be further torn.

"Hey!" a student yelled as I was sitting down in a corner alone. I turned in the direction of the sound and saw a boy about three years older than me speeding toward me. "Where are your shoes?" He nagged with a straight-face.

"I don't own shoes," I answered as I got up.

"You don't have shoes, is that right?" he mocked while shaking his head. "I'll give you a shoe, if I kick your ass with one."

I could feel anger building in my body, and my fingertips turned cold. My mouth quivered before I cleared my throat. "Please, man, just leave me alone. I don't want any trouble," I pleaded. *Control yourself, and keep calm*, I cautioned myself. Students began to surround us.

"Well, coward, you got yourself into some," he said, bringing himself up to his full height. He closed his right hand into a fist and slowly punched the inside of his other hand.

"Ooohhh, are you going to let him call you a coward?" someone from the crowd yelled. The bully was encouraged by the crowd's attention and moved so he was now up in my face.

"Yeah, Clesio, are you going to let me call you coward?" he taunted. I started losing my temper, so I turned to walk away. As I was walking out of the circle, someone pulled me back in.

"Fight! Fight! Fight!" everyone chanted.

The bully pushed my chest. "Do something about it," he insisted as he cracked his knuckles.

My blood turned to ice. "I told you, I don't want to fight."

"You don't have any choice," he said with a sinister smile. My patience was gone, but I was thinking of the consequences.

"Come on, kick his ass already," someone from the crowd encouraged him. I looked around to find a way to escape, but the circle was tight around us.

The bully began to take his shoes off. "How about I fight you?"

I instantly fell something snap in my body, and I lost it.

"You want to kick my ass, then kick my ass!" Before he could act, I punched him in the face. He dropped to the ground, and after a moment of stunned silence, the whole crowd began hitting me. Some were on top of me, punching me everywhere, while others were kicking me. I couldn't do anything, so I lay there, curling up my body as much as I could to dodge punches and kicks.

Teachers came about ten minutes later and split us apart.

"Stop fighting each other!" one the teachers commanded. But ultimately, they all turned and left the scene without bothering to resolve the issue or notice my bleeding face.

I did my best to clean up in the bathroom and sat through class until the end. When I got home, I threw my plastic bag into the bedroom and rushed to feed the animals, and by the time I returned home in the darkness, Mary never saw my bruised face.

The confrontation outside the classroom was not my only concern. I faced constant challenges inside as well. In Cape Verde, teachers were expected to discipline children; many parents, indeed, would even encourage teachers to hit their children when they misbehaved. Because there was no law against corporal punishment, teachers wouldn't get sanctioned or punished for abusing students. Commonly, they would use a wooden paddle with one end shaped exactly like the palm of a hand. The paddle had holes in the center so that welts would form when the paddle was used. Most of the time teachers would arrange our chairs in a circle, ask us questions, and if one student failed to answer, whoever answered it would hit the person ten times with the paddle. Then the teacher would hit the offender again with a long wooden stick.

Mary authorized my teacher Diana to utilize all means necessary to get me to learn, even though she never allowed me to study. Since I never had time to study, I didn't learn the material covered in class. As a result, more than any other student, I received beatings by students and the teachers. Sometimes, they would hit the inside of my hands so many times that I wouldn't be able to make a fist for days. Almost every day my hands would be swollen, and yet I was still expected to work with those hands.

Every day before class, Ms. Diana would call us one by one to check our homework. One day immediately after I sat down next to Felipe, on the third row, she began calling students, starting from the front row and working her way to the back. *Damn, she never fails with this stupid homework.* I looked at my swollen hands from the repeated beatings I endured and from working in the farm every day.

My heart accelerated faster and faster as she got closer and closer to me.

"Felipe, homework please!" Diana called firmly a moment later.

"I didn't do my homework," Felipe responded, hesitating.

"Well, you know the drill. Come here!"

He slowly walked to Diana's desk and extended his hand for Diana to hit with the wooden paddle.

My knees and hands shook uncontrollably while sweat trickled down my forehead as I watched Felipe receiving a beating that consisted often to twelve slaps. *Clesio, just tell her truth. No, if she tells Mary, I am toasted,* I debated as I pulled my hair.

"Clesio, homework please!"

I instantly froze. I quickly looked around and hesitated to stand up. Standing up, I opened my mouth, but nothing came out. I tried again. "I-I didn't do my homework because I didn't have time to do it," I mumbled.

"I can't hear you! Come over here!" Diana raised her voice. I forced my legs to work and lumbered to her desk. "What is wrong?"

Looking into her eyes, I knew no matter what I tell her, she wouldn't believe me. But desperate, I tried anyway.

"I never do my homework or study because I don't have time," I uttered softly.

"Why?" she asked as if she already knew the answer.

"Because I have to work all morning, and that is also the reason I am late most of the time."

She rolled her eyes while shaking her head as she reached for my right hand. "Stop making excuses." She raised her hand above her head and hit my swollen hand, leaving welts. "This will help you find time to study. When you feel your hand hurting, use it as a reminder to study hard because as you know, I have no problem hitting your hands until they fall off." She continued the beating.

"Please believe me, I'm telling the truth. Look at my hands. I have to work all day with these hands. They hurt." I cried. My hand turned red and enlarged until I couldn't close it.

"Give me the other hand," she demanded with joy, but before I could even act, she snatched my left hand and began hitting. With each hit, my hands felt as if they were sitting in boiling water.

When she finally decided to stop, I swiped tears with the back of my hands. I began walking to my desk, still holding my hands up in the air. Everyone stared in silence.

"I'm going to pass by this weekend, and I will confirm with Mary if you really work all day, or if you're just creating this charade."

I stopped instantly, turned, and walked back to her desk. "No, no, no, please don't do that. Please don't tell Mary. She will kill me," I pleaded.

"Clesio, I've heard that before, you lazy students making excuses for not studying. Go sit down," she ordered.

Two days later, I saw Diana walking toward our house with a sack of beans on top of her head. She owned a piece of land two minutes from us. *Here we go.* I quickly stopped sweeping, dropped the broom, and run to the bedroom to wear more clothing, knowing that I was about to get a ruthless beating. As I ran back outside, I spotted Mary curiously walking outside, trying to identify the person coming in our direction. Barefoot and with her ashy legs and arms, covered with scratch marks, she stepped closer to the edge of the porch and placed her right hand on her forehead to increase her focus.

"Is that Diana?" Mary asked, looking at me. Without a word, I shrugged and resumed sweeping.

"Hi, Mary!" Diana greeted Mary when she finally arrived.

She dropped the beans and sat at the bottom stair.

"I thought I recognize you from the distance." Mary smiled, descending the stairs and extended her hand to greet Diana. "Come inside."

"No, I'm fine right here. I'm not going to stay long. I have to go make dinner and correct some tests."

"What brought you here?"

Diana turned her head slightly to spy if I was listening, but I kept sweeping, pretending I wasn't. "Well, I'm here because of Clesio."

"What did he do this time?" Mary asked with exhaustion.

"Clesio is performing very poorly in school. He is not studying. He never does his homework, and he is blaming you. He told me he doesn't have time to study because he works all day long. Is that true?"

"Not at all. Really? I can't believe he would say such thing. The boy has some serious issues. I constantly tell him, 'Clesio, go study! Clesio, go study!' And he always says that he finishes all his studies, including his homework." She gave me an evil look, indicating that she was going to hit me as soon as Diana left. She then turned her head to Diana with a disappointed face as though she didn't know about my poor performance. "Clesio spends all day goofing around, doing nothing. If he isn't studying, that's only because he doesn't want to. Diana, as I already told you, you have my permission. Do whatever is necessary to get the boy to study."

My teacher nodded, agreeing with her. "Clesio, did you hear what Mary said? You better start studying if you don't want to get beaten at school," Diana said with a glowing smile. She got up, lifted the beans, and put them back on top of her head and left.

Immediately after Ms. Diana's departed, Mary sent me to find her favorite electric cord.

"What did I tell you about damaging my image in front of people? You are an embarrassment to this family. You always do something to destroy my reputation! And now you are going to pay," she said, glowering. "Go get the cord now!"

I plodded to the backyard, hid the cord under a pile of woods, and returned.

"I can't find it," I said expressionlessly, hoping she didn't detect the deception.

Her eyes widened in disappointment as she advanced toward me with increasing speed. She lunged through, knocking me out of her way, causing me to sprawl on my back, as she galloped to look for the cord herself.

"Useless!" she shouted.

Lifting my eyes toward the sky, I prayed, *Please, God, don't let her find the stupid cord*. A few minutes later, she returned with a piece of wood as wide as a baseball bat. *Oh man, you must be kidding me.*

I promptly took a few steps back. "Oh, I think I remember where your cord is!" I yelled, hesitating. She sped toward me viciously, carried me by my chest, and clenched her teeth.

"Do you think I'm playing with you?"

"No, no, of course not! I just remembered, and I thought you would like to know."

"Then go get it now!" Hopeless, I went to get the cord.

"Take your shirt off!" she demanded when I returned with the cord.

"What?" I asked, pretending as though I didn't hear her the first time. My blood turned cold, then hot as it rushed to my face.

"You heard me. Take your shirt off!" Shying away, I began to take my shirt off.

Suddenly, I heard, "Stop!" Catia had shouted and was now walking toward us. Instantly, Mary's mouth dropped in disbelief that Catia was challenging her. "Why are you always abusing that kid? What did he ever do to you?" she asked, as tears began rolling down her face.

"Because he always makes me look like an ass in public. Can you believe he told Diana that I am the reason he doesn't study? Me!"

"When does he have time to study? He spends most of his time working in the fields!" Mary's face turned red, knowing that Catia was right.

"Why don't you take care of your own business, and stay out of this if you don't want to be beaten with him?" said Mary, pointing the cord at Catia, signaling that she would hit her also.

Catia cleared her throat while reaching for me and hugged me close to her, acting as a shield. "Go ahead, Mary! You can start hitting me right now. Enough is enough! He is just a child, and he does everything around here despite your abuse. He doesn't deserve any of these. What else do you want?"

I could feel Catia's heart beating faster and faster as she spoke.

"I'm warning you. This is your last chance. Let him go."

Catia pulled me closer to her.

"Go on, hit us both."

Before she closed her mouth, Mary began hitting both of us, Catia receiving the most since her body was more exposed. After the beating, Catia went inside with her bruised back and cried.

Catia spent weeks in bed, suffering from back pain, while out on the farm, I would sneak away to find tejerinha, known for its healing powers. Hiding the plant in my pocket, I would boil it in the kitchen to make a liquid medicine. Sitting by Catia's bedside, I would dip my shirt in it and clean the cuts over her body from the cord. I would also give it to her to drink, trying to take away as much of her pain as possible. After dinner, I would bring her food and water, or her pipe if she asked for it. On the days she wanted to stand up and get out of bed, I would help her, despite my muscles already being weak from the day's work. During those weeks, I missed school several times to stay home to take care of her after I completed all my chores.

Despite all the dreadful experiences at school, I could hardly wait until school time because it was my only chance to escape the terror of Mary. Walking to school each day was like going to paradise—dealing with issues at school was better than dealing with Mary and her demands

CHAPTER 5

Life with Dogs

Dogs are truly our best friends. They have the ability to understand and communicate with humans. In Cape Verde, dogs are used mainly to protect property and herd animals. With their keen, intuitive senses, they sleep outside to alert people when they suspect a threat. They will bark until the owners wake up, and sometimes, they will even scare off intruders by themselves.

Well-trained dogs also help people herd their animals from place to place. Farm animals need to be moved for many reasons. First, it is unhealthy for animals to stay in one location for a long time because their excrement will accumulate and produce an odor that prevents them from eating. Second, during heavy rain, animals need to be moved to dry places.

During the rainy season, I had to wake up at 3:00 a.m., an hour earlier than my normal schedule, to move animals to uncultivated land so they could eat weeds. And at night, I had to bring them back to sleep in their shelters near the house. However, if it rained during the day, especially with heavy wind, I would have to move these animals back to their shelter immediately before floodwater carried them away. Transferring a large number of animals was really difficult, if not impossible, for a child to perform alone. It was also time-consuming because animals have a herd mentality; when one heads in the wrong direction, others will follow.

One day, I came from school and rushed to the backyard after I changed into my working clothing, when I noticed two little things playing with one another. One had four white legs and a white belly, while its back was black. Its face was brown, while its ears were half black and half brown.

Its little tail was a mix of black and while. The other one was black with golden-brown legs, neck, and belly.

The backyard was between the kitchen, the living room, and our bedroom. Mary used the left side to grow tobacco plants, but the right was only used for sitting. There were three rough wooden benches, placed on each corner. Catia was sitting on the bench near the kitchen, watching those things playing, while Mary sat near her tobacco plants, smoking her pipe.

"Oh, Clesio, you are home! Look at what I got you!" Catia said, pointing at those two little things.

Curiously, I rushed to them, and my mouth dropped as I got closer. "Are those poppies?"

"Yes. I bought them for you. I brought them for you." Catia smiled and turned one of the puppies toward me.

I knelt down, picked both up, and gently brought them to my chest. "They are cute! What can I name them?" I looked at Catia.

"Those animals are waiting for you to feed them!" Mary shouted while releasing pipe smoke into the air.

"Can you just let him play with them for a little bit?" Catia pleaded.

"No! Those things aren't going anywhere. He can play with them some other time."

I gently lowered the puppies to the ground. They followed me as I walked away. I stopped and turned to them. "Don't worry, I will be right back to you guys," I said in a baby voice. I picked them up again.

Mary instantly jumped and snatched those puppies out of my hands. "Go! Why do you always make me want to kill you?" she snapped. She pushed me as hard as she could.

Without a word, I headed to take care of the animals. I rushed through as fast as I could and returned home about an hour and a half later, approximately twenty minutes earlier than normal. But it was already dark outside by the time I finished.

Upon my arrival home, Mary and Catia were in the bedroom. Mary was sitting on the edge of their bed, smoking her pipe. The room was filled with smoke. Catia was sitting on a long wooden bench, located between my bed and theirs. Catia was combing her hair with her fingers. The puppies were sniffing around.

"You are back already!" Mary barked in disbelief. "I'm going to check those animals in the morning, and pray to God that I find them well fed."

"I fed them all." I took a couple of steps back, while ensuring she wasn't getting up.

"Okay, we will see tomorrow."

She put the pipe back in her mouth and looked away.

I sat on the floor right next to Catia. The puppies came between my legs. "You guys are so cute. Catia, what do we name them?"

"Wait and see what they like and then name them based on what they like."

"Okay," I agreed, coughing.

Suffocating, Catia opened the door, allowing smoke to exit the room.

A few weeks later, I named them Falido and Korioso. Falido means "someone who doesn't play with his or her food." Falido was a playful dog, but not when he was eating. He absolutely hated when I tried to play with him while eating. Although he wouldn't bite me, he would growl, indicating to leave him alone. Moreover, he wouldn't perform any task when he was hungry. Both Falido and Korioso learned our routine about herding animals. So when I whispered, "Let's go," they would follow me. But if Falido was hungry, he would refuse to go even when I ordered him; he would shake his head, indicating that he wasn't going.

One day, I tested him to see to what extent he would be stubborn, so I didn't feed him. When it was time to leave, I called him. He shook his head. I walked to him and tried to drag him, but he sat on the ground and dug in to prevent me from pulling him. After failing at this attempt several times, I fed him. As soon as he finished eating, he was the first to head out. Not surprisingly, on the days I had to stay on the field all day, he would leave me as soon as he was hungry, and only after Catia fed him would he then return to keep me company.

Korioso translates as "curious." Korioso, a very smart dog, liked to investigate. When he saw people in the far distance or noticed something unusual, he wouldn't stop barking or moving, until he figured it out. In addition, when I came home with any closed container, he would jump on me until I opened it, and if I left it unopened, he would manage to open it by himself.

Both dogs were fast learners; I began training them since they were puppies, and by the time they were a year old, they learned how to guide animals in a straight direction without frightening them or losing control. Since dogs work best when they are focused, I trained them separately to eliminate distraction and confusion. I trained Korioso to follow my whistle and Falido to follow my clap. For Korioso, one whistle meant "look at me," two meant "get your position," three meant "slow down the animals," four meant "abandon your position and help Falido," and five meant "reposition." Falido followed the same rules, but by claps. When working, I wouldn't play or talk to them because if they became distracted, they would frighten the animals, causing them to scatter in different directions.

When moving animals, each dog was responsible for its tasks. Korioso would take the front and Falido the middle, while I would stay in the back to oversee everything. If any animal moved from the line, Falido would cautiously exit the line without disturbing the rest and redirect the stray back into line. While Falido was redirecting the animal, Korioso would slow down the rest of the animals so we could keep all of them together.

Every time we moved animals successfully, I would pat them on their heads and say, "Good job," and they would wag their tails and jump to hug me. In fact, Korioso would get mad if I failed to compliment him. Refusing to take a step, he would sit until I patted him and said, "Good job." As soon as I did, he would wag his tail in excitement. I could tell he was proud to accomplish his tasks. Sometimes he would just jump on me with much force, causing me to fall.

Besides herding large animals, my dogs could also help control chickens. They would help me run after the chickens, allowing me to run until they figured out which one was the target. Then they would run after the specific chicken. To avoid injuring the chickens, they would lie on top of them instead of pouncing on them, and wait for me.

Korioso and Falido became more than my assistants; they became part of me. They became my best friends—my only friends, in fact. They were the only ones that cared about me besides Catia. We would play together after we transferred the animals. We would run against each other, and they would give me the advantage since they could run faster. They loved it when they won and hated when I did. When Falido lost, he would provoke me to run until he won.

As a result, we became very attached to each other. They wouldn't allow anyone to touch me, not even Mary. One time, they attacked Mary and bit her because she hit me with an electric cord. Thus, Mary had to tie them every time she planned to hit me because they would protect me. Every time my dogs were tied, I knew I was going to be beaten.

Although Falido was my favorite, Korioso showed me more affection. He was always by my side. He would even feel my pain. When Mary hit me or when I was sad, he would also be sad and would not eat until I ate or saw that I was okay. Moreover, he would get worried when he didn't know my whereabouts. He would accompany me halfway to school and return to walk me back home when I got out of school. He, in fact, loved to be around me, especially in the season when I had to sleep outside to protect our goats.

In the season when the wild dogs eat goats, I had to sleep in the fields to protect our goats. I hated to sleep outside, but Falido and Korioso loved the idea. In the season when wild dogs didn't attack goats and I didn't have to sleep outside, my dogs wanted to sleep inside with me. They would cry when I forced them to sleep out. When we would sleep outside, I didn't even have to call them because as soon as they saw me wearing my little sweater at night, they knew my destination, and they would lead the way.

Falido would sleep near my head, and Korioso would refuse to sleep apart. He loved to cuddle with me, and I had to hug him because if I didn't, he would wait until I fell asleep and sleep on top of me.

Many times Falido, Korioso, and I had to sleep outside, in the rain, during high wind, and even in the storms to protect our goats. We would take turns keeping vigilance. Falido was a heavy sleeper, so he would watch first, and then I would take the watch until Korioso woke up. Korioso would then stay up until morning. When they detected wild dogs approaching from a distance, they would pull my shoulder to wake me up. They wouldn't bark to avoid drawing the wild dogs' attention. They would wake me up just in case the wild dogs decided to cross over to our territory. Falido and Korioso would stay quiet and still until I said, "Attack."

Some nights the wild dogs wouldn't even reach us, or if they did, we would scare them away. But some nights it was difficult to prevent the killing because the wild dogs traveled in packs. When they did, I had to help my dogs fight these abusive dogs.

One day, a group of eight dogs stalked our goats, and my dogs and I tried our best to prevent them from killing the goats. I ordered Falido and Korioso to attack. Falido fought any wild dogs that were trying to attack the goats, while Korioso and I tried to frighten them away. Korioso always fought near me so if anything went wrong, he would be able to help me. Falido was fighting two wild dogs, and Korioso and I were fighting six.

I was able to kill one wild dog before my stick broke. Then other wild dogs noticed that I was vulnerable without my stick, and they began to attack me instead of the goats. Immediately after my stick broke, Korioso moved in front of me, protecting me. Falido also abandoned the goats and cut over to me. I quickly realized there were more wild dogs than we could handle, and it was impossible to save the goats. I acknowledged I was in a great danger of being killed, so I attempted to stampede. While I was trying to escape, Falido and Korioso were intercepting the wild dogs to slow them down. But because I was only nine years old, those dogs could stampede faster than me.

After running for about three minutes, exhausted, I tripped and fell. The wild dogs were on top of me. I put my arms up to protect my face. One wild dog leapt and landed on my stomach, sharp claws ripping into the skin all over my arms. Another one had grabbed my shirt, trying to get at my side. I cried out as strong jaws clamped on my ankle, trying to drag me away from the other two. I could feel them trying to tear me apart, my skin breaking, and the metallic smell of blood riddled my nose. Dirt kicked up into my eyes, and my ears were ringing with their snarls. I tried to fight back, kicking at the dog on my ankle. I swung at the dog on top of me and hit it under its jaw. It rolled off, and I turned, trying to get my arms under me so I could start running again. The dog at my side took its chance and latched on to my shoulder. I cried out, trying to punch him off. The other dog regained his footing and started lunging at me again. I kept swinging my arms wildly, trying to keep them away. . .

Falido and Korioso were also in trouble, so they couldn't help me. But several minutes later, Korioso and Falido broke free and reached me. Korioso pushed two of the wild dogs off, me while I kicked the third off, and Falido pulled me up by my shoulder, helping me to my feet. Once I was standing, Korioso and Falido blocked the dogs' way, while I ran to climb a tree.

The fighting continued as I was sitting in the tree. Watching my two dogs getting killed was even more painful than the wild dogs' bites. Falido and Korioso were sacrificing their lives to save mine and the goats'. *I can't let them die. If Falido and Korioso die, I might as well die with them. They are my closest friends. They are the only ones who make me smile and distract me from my problems.*

Deciding to rescue them, I took a deep breath and gathered my courage before attempting to break a piece of a branch to use as a weapon. A sudden strong wind pushed me too far out to the edge, and the branch broke unexpectedly, and I sprawled to the ground. Two wild dogs attacked me immediately. Knowing that I didn't have enough time to get to my feet, I made a critical decision—fight bare-handed. I punched one of the dogs hard on the ear, knocking it out for a couple of minutes, which allowed me to fight the other dog. The dog was on top, trying to bite my face; I blocked my face with my two hands. It tore a piece of skin from my elbow. I howled out in pain. Then I managed to get on top and reached for a rock. With frustration, I repeatedly hit the rock against its head while screaming, "Leave us alone! Leave us alone! Leave us alone!" I felt warm blood splashing onto my face, eyes, and arms with every hit. I paused and wiped blood from my face, leaving traces of blood all over. Placing my two hands around its neck, I pressed as hard as I could. I felt it slowly vibrate to its death between my tiny hands.

I grabbed the broken branch and helped my two dogs fight. After fighting for nearly ten minutes, I injured two more wild dogs, and the other four, including the one I punched on the ear, ran away. But I was too late.

Korioso, Falido, and I were seriously injured. Korioso could hardly walk, and while I carried him home, I could hear him breathing heavily.

"Korioso, please don't die. Stay with me. You cannot die." My black shirt was covered with blood. He raised his head and looked into my eyes for a few seconds. I could see the sadness in his eyes—not the sadness of death but of leaving someone he loved behind. I could sense he was worried about who was going to take care of me. He slowly closed his eyes. I tried to run home, but he died in my arms before I arrived home.

"No, no, no, no, noooo, don't die! I really need you. Who is going to take care of me?" I said, crying. "Please don't die. You can't do this to me. Who is going to walk me to school now?" Falido walked and sat near my feet. I rested Korioso down and hugged both of them. I desperately wished I could bring him back and alter the events. "Falido, what are we going to do now?"

Then I noticed that Falido was shaking uncontrollably. He had bites on his neck, legs, tail, and back. Half of both his ears were torn off. He was shaking and limping. His face was covered with blood. When I looked in his eyes, his head dropped. I could tell he wasn't only sad but also in pain.

"I'm so sorry, Falido. Don't worry, I'm here for you. I will take care of you, and I won't let you die," I said, fearing that I was wrong. After I cried hopelessly for about fifteen minutes, Falido and I headed home. Every morning, he would go straight to the kitchen, looking for food. Today, instead, he lay under a tree near the water tank. I began panicking. Losing Korioso was bad enough; I couldn't bear to lose Falido too.

He needed treatment immediately, yet there was no hospital or clinic that treated animals anywhere near. Without Mary's permission, I ran to the only clinic in the area, about five miles away, attempting to obtain medicine for Falido. Although I was seriously injured and covered in blood, I waited three hours before I was serviced.

"Next!" the doctor yelled. Half asleep, I went in. The doctor's mouth dropped instantly when he saw me. "Are you okay? What happened?"

"I'm fine, but my dog is not," I said as I sat down. "Can you please give me something to treat my dog's wounds?"

"No, I can't give you medicine for your dog, but I will treat you," he said. A million thoughts cluttered my head. *What am I going to do now? Am I supposed let Falido die? What am I going to tell Mary about my long disappearance?*

I knew for sure I was going to be beaten when I arrived home, but I couldn't let the only creature I loved die.

"You don't have to treat me. I'm fine. Please just give me some medicine to treat my dog."

"I told you, I cannot do that," he refused. I shook my head, stood up, and trotted out.

"I still need to treat you. Come back," said the doctor while running after me.

I stopped and turned around before screaming, "I told you I don't need help. I'm fine!" I burst into tears.

"Okay, okay, okay . . . Come back and I will give you something for your dog." Suddenly I could see clearly, and hope began building in my heart. "This is your lucky day. I'm going to treat you as well as give you medicine for your dog." He smiled. *If I have two lucky days like this, I will be dead.* After the treatment, I ran home, only to find Mary waiting for me on the porch with the electric cord.

"Where have you been?" she barked.

"I went to the clinic," I said firmly. Although I knew I was going to be beaten, I wasn't afraid. I was only thinking about Falido, so I went straight to my dog.

"Look at me when I talk to you! Where are you going?" I could hear her heavy stomps following me.

"To treat Falido."

"No, you are not. You are late for feeding the animals."

"I will go as soon as I finish."

Mary began hitting me as I knelt down to clean Falido's wounds. Although she was slicing my back, I didn't stop the treatment or even care about the beating. She got angry because my attention was fully concentrated on Falido. My back felt as if its skin was ripped apart by the time she finished.

"Let me leave you before I kill you," she said with a hint of surrender in her voice.

I continued treating Falido until I finished and then headed out to feed the animals.

All I could think about was whether or not Falido would live. I rushed through everything so I could come home as soon as possible to check up on Falido. Unaware of my steps, I hit my toe against a rock so hard that my nail almost came off. I wasn't wearing shoes, of course. I cried over the pain for about a minute, peeled-off the remaining skin, and finished my tasks, only thinking about Falido's well-being.

Uncaring about my injuries, or my dog's, Mary hit me again after she learned the consequences of the attack. My inability to fight off the wild dogs allowed them to kill two baby goats and one adult goat. Because I couldn't save these animals, despite my bleeding from her first beating, the bites from the wild dogs, and my ripped off toenail, she beat me again with the stupid electric cord.

I tried everything I could to save Falido, but it wasn't enough. Two days later, when I returned home from school, I found Falido dead. I dropped to the ground, not believing my eyes or wanting to accept the reality. Everything went black, and suddenly nothing had meaning. It felt like the world had just ended.

Food wouldn't even pass down my throat. The deaths of Falido and Korioso touched me deeply in a way I had never been touched before, despite the devastation when I learned that my grandmother passed away. Waking up in the morning not having them to meet me by the door was heartbreaking. Besides my grandmother and mother, these two amazing dogs were the only living beings I ever loved, and now they were gone. Once again, I was left in the world without hope. What am I going to do now? Who is going to distract me from my pain? Who is going to comfort me? Who is going to protect me now?

If my life was painful, at least it wasn't depressing until now.

CHAPTER 6

A Lonely Life

After Falido's and Korioso's deaths, my life became more miserable than ever. Without my dogs to distract me from my problems, I was terribly lonely. When I was working in the fields, I would often feel as if no one cared about me besides my mother and my grandmother. I would stop working for a moment and look around, but there was nothing else to see. The lack of connection would make me feel hopeless, with no reason to live. Many times, I wished I had someone to talk to about my fears and worries because when I was isolated from people, I would often think about committing suicide.

I remember repeatedly standing on the edge of a cliff about seventy feet high and slowly taking steps toward the edge. Hesitating, I would look down and close my eyes, leaning over the edge, hoping the wind would push me off. *Don't be a coward, jump already*, I would encourage myself. But every time, I would hear another voice saying, "Don't do it. Please don't do it."

One day, I even felt as if someone was pulling me backward, causing me to fall on my back. I immediately began crying as I lay there, thinking about my mother and how painful it would be for her to lose a son—she might even blame herself for not being there for me. She didn't deserve to experience such a horrible feeling.

Still lying on the ground, I wondered how amazing living with my mother would be—if just talking to her would bring me joy, imagine living with her. I thought how wonderful it would be to have my mother tuck me into bed, kiss me good night, and make me breakfast each morning. With my mother I would live a normal life, a life without pain. I wouldn't suffer anymore, I wouldn't have to work as a slave anymore, and I wouldn't be abused. I would be with someone who loves me, someone who would take care of me, and spend time with me, taking me places, so I didn't have to be alone.

Still lying, I thought about who would take care of my mother if I committed suicide. I wanted to be there to help and project her. Knowing that my mother would struggle to survive worried and hurt me deeply. I wanted to grow up and have a job in order to take care of her so she wouldn't have to work ever again. I always dreamed of being successful in life, not only to make my mother proud, but also to be able to look her in the eye and tell her that I would provide everything. I wished one day, my mother would hug me and whisper in my ear that she was proud of me.

Then I realized I couldn't commit suicide because I desperately wanted my dreams to come true. Instead of daydreaming about how wonderful it would be to live with my mother, I wanted to go to bed and wake up in my mother's arms and hear her say, "I love you, my son." Although I had heard these words over the phone before, I wanted her to tell me in person. Thinking about my mother was the only thing keeping me from committing suicide.

Even though it would sometimes take as long as six months before I would speak to my mother, on the phone, her voice gave me reasons and purposes to live.

There was only one phone in my area, about twenty minutes away, and it was owned by Maria. My mother would call Maria in advance and then call back an hour later, giving Maria enough time to send someone to call me. My mother was the only one to initiate the calls, but the majority of the time, she wouldn't be able to reach me because I would be working in the fields, or even when I was at home, Mary would just tell the messenger I wasn't available. Whenever she decided to allow me to talk to my mother, Mary would always go with me to ensure I didn't talk about the maltreatment.

"You must be excited," Mary said to break the awkward silence as we walked to Maria's house.

"Yes, I'm," I said, trying not to reveal my true excitement.

"You don't have to tell your mother what goes on in the house, you know. Mothers get worried easily, and you don't want your mother to worry for nothing," she said with an unreadable face.

"I'm not going to." There was a long pause.

"When are you going to finish digging? You have to finish it as soon as possible because it will rain anytime."

"I don't know, but I will make sure I finish it soon," I said, getting aggravated.

"Have you fed the animals?"

"I have in the morning, but I haven't had a chance to feed them again. I was digging all day."

"Right. Just make sure you feed them when we get back," she uttered, breathing heavily. I began to walk fast to avoid the conversation. "Why are walking so you fast? Wait for me!" she yelled. I reduced my speed. "You have no manners. You are supposed to walk behind me so you protect me. But I guess the world has changed. In my time, men were romantic and respectful, and they wouldn't leave a woman behind." *I wonder why they left you behind.* She continued talking, but all I could hear was my mother's voice.

We arrived at Maria's house shortly after.

While talking to my mother on the phone, I always imagined how wonderful it would feel to fall asleep in her arms as she read me a bedtime story. But because I knew she was struggling on her own to survive each day, I wouldn't reveal my feelings.

"Hello, hello, Clesio?" my mother said.

"Hi," I replied.

"How are you?"

"I'm good."

"How is Mary treating you?" I paused and looked at Mary. Mary instantly got closer to me so she could hear the conversation.

"She's treating me good."

"She isn't hitting you, right?" I clenched my teeth, fighting my true emotion.

"No, she doesn't."

"Are you going to school?"

"Yes."

"Are you getting good grades?"

"Yes," I lied so she wouldn't learn about the abuse and the hard labor. "How are you?"

"I'm good," she answered in a happy voice.

"When are you coming to visit me?"

"I'm not sure yet, but I will make sure I come soon. Do you know Mom . . ." She hesitated over the next word. "Mom misses you so much?" Tears filled my eyes, but I took a moment to hide my feelings. I didn't want her to worry about me.

"I miss you, too," I said, smiling so I could sound happy. Mary tapped her wrist, indicating that time was up. "We have to go now before it's too dark out," I lied as Mary gave me a thumbs-up.

"Okay, it is so nice hearing your voice again. Be safe and behave."

"Okay, I will. Bye. I love you."

"I love you, too." I could tell she was heartbroken just as I was.

I handed the phone to Mary. I could hear only what Mary was saying.

"Clesio is doing fine. He is a nice boy. We have a lot of fun together." *I hope your tongue falls off.* "Bye now. It was nice talking to you, and you don't have to worry. I will take good care of Clesio."

Mary was happy I protected her reputation with my mother. On the way home, she tried to engage in a conversation with me.

"Your mother seemed distant. She doesn't seem like she misses you," Mary said as though she cared about me. "But don't worry, my mother and I care about you."

"I know. You guys are the only ones I need," I responded sarcastically. She laughed and wrapped her arm awkwardly around my neck. I began to feel uncomfortable.

"We will live together forever, right?"

"For . . . eveeer?" *Oh Lord, please help me. Don't let this happen.*

"What? Don't you like to live with us forever?"

"Oh, of course, I would love to live with you guys foooreveeeeer."

I pretended to check the bottom of my feet so she would unwrap her arm around my neck. She stopped to wait until I finished. I then walked past her to avoid the hugging. I could see she was thrilled about my willingness to live with her. At least she thought I was willing to stay. The discomfort lasted until we arrived home.

"Clesio!" she called loudly as I left to feed the animals. My heart dropped. *What did I do now?*

"Yes?" I answered, turning my head toward her to see if she had the electric cord.

"Where are you going?" My eyes widened because she knew my routine.

"Feeding the animals," I responded, confused.

"It is okay. You don't have to feed them tonight. You are tired. You have been working all day. Come on! Come and rest." She extended her arm, signaling me to return.

Skeptical, I turned around and sat on the porch. Mary sat beside me, wrapped her arm around my shoulders, and gently pulled me towards her. I could smell the strong scent of pipe smoke on her clothes, and I began to feel suffocated.

"This is nice. We are spending time together." I nodded. "We are so busy. We barely spend any time together."

I thank God for that. "Yeah." *How can I get out of here?* The time felt as if it weren't moving.

"You are a nice kid, you know that?" *Oh, maybe that's why you constantly abuse me. What does this woman want?* She looked at me, so I threw her a fake smile. "Your mother should be proud of you. I don't understand her."

"I don't understand her either. What a strange woman!"

Hesitating, I removed her arm from my shoulders and leaned forward, pretending to examine my injured toe.

"What happened there?"

"I hit my toe against a rock."

"When did this happen?"

"The day the wild dogs killed our goats."

"Those stupid dogs." *Do you mean the stupid Mary?*

"Yeah, those stupid dogs." I stood up and walked around the water tank.

"Where are you going?" she asked as she slowly followed me. *Damn, I cannot catch a break.*

"Washing my feet so I can go to bed." She caught up with me and placed her hand on my back.

"Why so early?"

"I'm tired, and I have to wake up early in the morning." She jumped in front of me as I attempted to grab a bucket of water on top of the water tank.

"Let me help you." She poured water into my wash container. *Am I dreaming? This is so weird.*

"Where is Catia?" I said, hoping she would go look for her.

"I don't know."

"Do you want me to go look for her?"

"No, it is okay. You are washing your feet. I will go look for her. Maybe she is in the kitchen."

"Okay."

"Don't forget to eat something before you go to bed!" she shouted across the water tank as she headed to the kitchen. I took a deep breath after she left. *What the heck is happening? Is the world finally coming to an end?*

A few minutes after I washed my feet, I went to bed without eating.

Not surprisingly, the kindness didn't last. Mary woke me up at 3:00 a.m. instead of 4:00 a.m. to feed the animals since they hadn't had dinner.

"Clesio, Clesio, wake up, wake up," Mary demanded. I lay there pretending I didn't hear her. "Clesio, get up now. Don't make me go over there."

And she is back. "What time is it?" I asked, half asleep.

"It's 3:00 a.m."

"I still have an hour," I said, frustrated.

"No, you don't!" she yelled. "Those poor animals, you didn't even feed them last night. Get up, get up."

"They waited all night. Can't they wait one more hour? Plus it's dark out. How am I supposed to see?"

She got up and grabbed me by the chest and dragged me out of bed.

"When I talk to you, you don't challenge me." I immediately ran outside to avoid a beating.

At these difficult times, remembering my mother's voice kept my spirit indomitable. She would give me the strength to overcome Mary's abuse and any other obstacle in life. My mother's voice was the medicine I needed to heal all my pains because I knew one day I would be with her. It made me feel strong and alive. Though the phone conversation would intensify my urge to be with her instantly, which would make me cry and miss her even more, it did help me heal some of my pain.

CHAPTER 7

Saying Goodbye and Reuniting

In 2002, my father visited Cape Verde, and during his stay, he came to my school to meet me. Although it was my first time seeing him, my first words were "Please help me move out of Mary's house!"

My father was agreeable. "I think that's a good idea. Since you, your sister, and your brother are going to America soon, moving together would allow you to get to know each other." I could tell, though, he was surprised by the urgency of my request.

A week later, my father came to Mary's to pick me up. I was cleaning the backyard.

"Clesio, I think your father is here," Catia said with a surprised tone in her voice. My heart pounded. I was fearful that Mary and my father might get into a confrontation. I dusted off my jeans, T-shirt, and face and followed Catia to the front porch, where my father and Mary were already standing.

"Hey, big boy, how are you?" my father asked, hugging me.

"I'm good."

"Go get ready. I'm taking you to São Jorge to live with your brother and sister."

Mary's eyes widened. "He cannot go without his mother's permission," she interjected, frustrated.

"Mary, I didn't come here to ask for permission," my father raised his voice. He turned to me and again told me to get ready. "I have to go soon."

"Mary, let him go. Let his mother worry about him," Catia coaxed. Disappointed, Mary sat on a concrete bench.

"Okay, but I know this isn't over," Mary said firmly.

My father and I left immediately after. Walking away from the house felt magical—no more isolation and no more abuse.

We walked, me leading the way to the road where my father had parked his car.

"That woman is weird and frightening. To be honest, I was a little scared of her," my father admitted.

"Tell me about it," I replied with a wry smile.

"How did you put up with her all these years?"

"I really don't know. I just live one day at a time."

He smiled. "That's all over now. Are you excited about living with your siblings?"

"Yes. I've always wanted to be with them. One time, Nelson and Neminha came to take me to spend a weekend with them, but Mary refused to let me go."

"Why?"

"Because I had to work and take care of the animals."

My father chuckled. "I'd like to see who will work for her now."

"I don't know, and I don't care. How am I going to continue my education from São Jorge?"

"You are going to temporary stay at my wife Linda's house until you finish this school year, and next year, you will go to school in São Jorge. Linda is in the United States, but you will stay with her mother and two siblings."

"Where is Linda's house?"

"It's about forty-five minutes walking from Mary's house. It is closer to school than Mary's house."

"Oh, that's good. When I move to São Jorge, who will I live with besides Neminha and Nelson?"

"With your aunt Bety at my mother's house."

"Is Grandmother there?"

"No, she's in the United States, but she comes and goes."

We arrived at Linda's house around eleven in the morning, and Linda's mother met me outside and hugged me. She had already prepared me breakfast. Right after breakfast, my father called me into a bedroom to give me presents he had brought from the United States. I ran to him, and he handed me a pile of new clothes. Jeans, T-shirts, new shoes, and also new school supplies. *Wow, wait until those jerks at school see the new me.*

Excited, I got ready and rushed off to school a little before noon, an hour earlier than when I was at Mary's. I could barely wait to go school with my new outfits and supplies. Everyone commented how beautiful my backpack and outfit were. For the first time, other students didn't pick on me. Instead of harassing me, they invited me to play games with them. Little did I know what to expect.

Later that day, to my shock and horror, Mary arrived to pick me up from school. "Excuse me, I'm here to pick up Clesio," she said as she stood in the doorway of my classroom. As soon as I heard her voice, my heart began beating rapidity, and my body started to shake. *God, please don't let this woman take me, please. Not again.* All the students and the teacher stared at Mary.

"But we are in the middle of class," the teacher told her. Mary then took about three steps into the room and put a fake smile on her face.

"He needs to see his mother right now." I got up instantly.

"My mother is here?" My pulse began to slow down.

Mary smiled. "Not here, silly. She's at home." She walked up to me and grabbed my hand. "Let's go." As soon as we exited the classroom, she began dragging me. She walked at a faster pace than I was able to, so she pushed me even when I got so tired. I could barely walk. I became suspicious.

"Is my mother home?" I asked between breaths.

"Keep walking."

"I'm tired. Can I please slow down?" I gasped. She stopped and frowned at me.

"Don't make me kill you right here." She pushed me in front of her. "Walk, walk." She grabbed a stick and poked me with it every time I slowed down.

Upon our arrival at home, she punched my stomach. "If your father comes, you better tell him you don't want to go if you don't want me to smash your head against the wall."

But I knew my father would come for me, and he would take me back with him. I was confident that Mary's abuse was coming to an end.

Approximately two hours later, my father arrived, furious. Mary promptly ran outside and stood in front of him, blocking his way.

"His mother said he can stay until he finishes school."

My father clenched his teeth. "Don't you ever come near my son again! You have no right to go drag him out of school!" My mouth dropped in disbelief. Catia could see the radiant expression on my face. She winked at me, and I threw her a smile over my shoulder. "Clesio, get your belongings, and let's go right now."

As I stood up, Mary grasped my wrist. "You cannot go!" She was wild-eyed. My father's face turned red.

"Let him go. I don't want to be violent, but I will if I have to," he said fiercely.

"Mary, let him go," Catia said, afraid. Mary released my hand.

"His mother isn't going to be happy about this."

"Let me make something clear here. If you come close to my son one more time, I am going to break your other arm. Let me worry about his mother." My father reached for my hand. As we were walking down the stairs, my father stopped and then strode over to Mary. She stepped back as he advanced. "He's still going to the same school, and if you go near him, it will not be just talking next time." I felt a huge release as we walked away.

"Are you sure she won't get me again?"

"I don't think so. She looked pretty scared. But don't worry. If she does, I will always come back for you."

As my father and I left the premises, I took a last look around and smiled. I felt free for the first time in ten years.

CHAPTER 8

Aunt Bety Seems Transformed

In June 2002, when I was fifteen, I moved to São Jorge to live at my grandmother's house with my aunt Bety. São Jorge is divided into two villages—main São Jorge and Kemadinha. Kemadinha, which means "little burn," was named after the volcano lava that flowed and left scorched rocks behind. The little area that the lava didn't reach was covered with dry, rocky soil, supporting only a few scrubby trees and withered grass. In Kemadinha, houses were few and randomly placed. Maybe twenty-five houses comprised the whole village. They had flat roofs and were located far from the road. Paths crisscrossed among the houses.

My grandmother's house, located in the village of Kemadinha, was about five minutes from the road, on a hill dead center between Jusefa's house about twenty feet up the hill and Agenelo's house about thirty feet down the hill. Agenelo, whom everyone called Dono (which translates as "grandfather"), was one of the oldest citizens of São Jorge. A family known as Mama Di Djunzi owned a house about ten feet in front of my grandmother's house.

Although my grandmother's house wasn't attractive, it was tenfold better than Mary's house. The exterior of my grandmother's house was green plastered stone and surrounded by plants. Its floor was also paved to look like tiles with clear beer bottles inserted bottom up in the cement to look like green-yellow jewels. A few of the bottoms were broken. Immediately outside the door was the water tank, which held about ten thousand gallons of water. The kitchen was attached to the house, but its entrance was from the outside. Adjacent to the kitchen were three bedrooms, each accessible from the outside. However, one also could walk through the bedrooms from within, like passing through the cars of a train. At the end of the third bedroom was a large living room.

Aunt Bety, mother of two-year-old Matio, had custody of my seventeen-year-old brother Nelson and my eighteen-year-old sister Neminha.

Nelson, with a round-faced and a chocolate skin color, was an outgoing person and liked to repair any broken items. Well, he broke more items than he repaired, but he enjoyed the process of disassembling and reassembling.

Bety was skinny and had long black hair. She suffered from asthma, so even the smallest walk would cause her to wheeze or use her pump. Bety, in her late twenties, had two moods—sweet and sour. She was sweet when people were present and sour when no one was watching. She went out of her way to make people believe she was sweet all the time.

When I first moved in, especially while my father was still visiting, Bety was friendly and loving. Since I was struggling to adapt to my new environment, she would give me tours of the neighborhood, and because I lacked people skills, she would even invite other neighborhood children to play with me. Though I didn't know how to socialize, it felt good spending time playing with other kids without worrying about working as at Mary's. Bety's display of affection made me believe she actually cared about me, but the fun didn't last long. I soon discovered her dark side. The only reason for the loving hostess treatment was to impress my father. As soon as he departed for the United States, everything changed.

For two months, life with Bety was magical, but the moment my father left, the "sour" Bety transformation became permanent. My brother and I became responsible for performing all the farm chores, such as digging holes, fertilizing the fields, and *monda*, which means taking care of the full process of growing. Once the cultivated plants grew about three inches tall, we would start removing the weeds. Little mounds of soil would be banked around each plant to prevent heavy rains from washing it away. Bety began to demand that Nelson and I work from 9:00 a.m. to 6:00 p.m. and then search for plants to feed the animals. When I was attending school, from October to May, I would be responsible for feeding the animals because Nelson would be working in the fields in the morning.

While my brother and I toiled in the fields, my sister Neminha, who had short hair, which she kept in ponytails most of the time, was responsible for all the house chores. She had to do laundry by hand for everyone, including our other aunt Eloisa and Eloisa's three children. In addition, Neminha had to prepare meals and clean the whole house.

My sister was on a tight leash, even when my sister turned twenty years old, she wasn't permitted to go anywhere. Nor was she allowed to have a boyfriend. Every time she spoke with a young man, even as friends, she would be beaten. She was beaten many times for actions she didn't commit. One night, she was talking to our neighbor Bruno, a young man about Neminha's age, and Jacira, Eloisa's daughter, wrongly accused her, reporting to Bety that Neminha and Bruno were kissing. Without investigating the truth, Bety ran outside and started beating Neminha.

One Saturday, I was playing soccer at Mama Di Djunzi's yard with Nelson, my friend Maruka, and my cousins Jelson and Steven.

"Someone is yelling your name, Clesio," Maruka told me. I ran toward our house, and as I turned the corner of Mama Di Djunzi's house, I saw Bety striding toward me.

"Fidju da puta! Can't you hear me calling you?" Bety snapped.

"I didn't hear you. I was playing soccer," I said, afraid but angry. I walked past her. She grabbed my hand and pulled me to her. Her eyes widened as she clenched her teeth. As soon as she touched me, I felt my blood run cold, a feeling familiar from my life with Mary.

"Okay, what's it?" I asked.

"Go collect plants to feed the animals." She pointed toward the fields.

"But I'm tired. I just got home from working in the field." I took a deep breath.

"What? Do you think these poor animals are going to sleep without food?"

Maybe not if you feed them yourself.

I plodded around the house until I was out of view and growled in frustration. I kicked at a piece of wood but hit a large rock instead. Limping on one foot, wincing, I grabbed the painful one. *Damn! I really need to stop kicking stuff . . . This is bullshit. I moved here for a better life, but I am right back where I began. At least at Mary's I didn't have friends to leave behind in the middle of the game.*

Feeding the animals in the green season was easy, but in the dry season, it became extremely hard to find enough plants for five adult and two baby goats. Everyone in the small community would be searching for plants to feed their animals, so by the middle of the season, plants would be scarce. The only ones available were on dangerous cliffs or in unreachable places.

Bety never seemed to accept this fact. She always expected me to bring more plants than I could find. If I failed to meet her expectations, she wouldn't only beat me but also send me back to search for more.

That day, I spent three hours searching for plants, but I could find very few. When I returned home with a little bundle on my head, Bety immediately shook her head and sent me back for more. I dropped the result of my hard labor in front of her and turned around to repeat the futile process.

Bety's abuse was getting worse every day. Three months later, I arrived from school at around 4:00 p.m., and without even a chance to eat, she sent me to pick a full sack of beans. To avoid confrontation, I instantly changed into my dirty jeans and baggy sweater and headed out to the beans field while my stomach growled throughout the way. I filled the sack by around 6:00 p.m., and when I tried to carry it, I realized it was heavier than I had anticipated. Nevertheless, I struggled and carried it home. As I was arriving with the bag on my head, I saw Bety sitting down on the porch, waving a piece of paper to cool herself.

"Can't you walk any faster?" Bety asked.

"I'm walking as fast as I can. These beans are heavy," I answered, breathing heavily.

"I don't care. Remember you still have to feed the animals." Without catching my breath, I dropped the beans in front of her and wobbled for a field I hadn't yet tried. I needed enough to feed our own goats as well as Eloisa's.

After walking for about twenty minutes, I spotted several plants on a high cliff. *Wow, they are so beautiful.* I looked up and realized the only reason the plants were still there was because the cliff was too dangerous to climb. No one had ever attempted to climb it, or if someone had, they had been unsuccessful. The cliff was about eighty feet high, and at its bottom lay large ragged rocks. *Clesio, climbing the cliff is a suicide mission. However, if you keep searching, you may not find enough plants, so Bety will beat you and send you back for more. If you climb and get those plants successfully, then she will have no reason to beat you, and if you climb you it and fall, you will die. Therefore, she will not have a chance to beat you up either.*

I decided to climb the cliff, even though my muscles were already tired from carrying the heavy bag of beans. As I pulled myself up the cliff, my arms grew weaker and weaker. *Come on. You can do this.* Halfway, I could feel my muscles burning, and suddenly I lost my grip. Now, I was holding on with only my left hand. My muscles wilted with the effort. *Don't look down, don't look down, don't look down.* Each second was critical because I had to regain my hold before my left arm got too weak to support my body. To prevent falling, I pushed myself as hard as I could as I felt my muscles stretching and burning. *Come on, Clesio, almost there.* Then I strained my muscles until I felt they would tear. After a minute of struggling and fighting, my right hand found a rock to grip, and I completed the second half of the climb.

Once on top, I rushed, gathering as many plants as possible to begin the climb down before dark. Distracted, I stepped on a loose rock, lost my balance, and started to tumble. While rolling toward the edge of the cliff, I tried to grab on to anything, but there was nothing to grip. *That's it. I'm going to die.* Feeling sharp pain on my head, back, and knee as I rolled down until reached an inch from falling off the cliff, I landed wedged between two rocks. Instead of getting up and leaving, I lay there and cried. After a minute, I noticed that if I inched carefully, I could reach an area where I could crawl my way back up. "Oh yeah, I'm not going to die!" I screamed. But before I even closed my mouth, a huge rock, the size of a car tire, worked loose and started heading directly toward me. There was nothing I could do because if I moved quickly, I would fall over the edge. Once again I thought of death. Because I couldn't do anything, I closed my eyes and waited for the rock to crush me.

As the rock rolled down, it gained speed. The rock passed about an inch across my body and knocked away one of the rocks I was lying in between. I fell off the cliff, and while falling, my heart dropped, causing me to suffocate. I tried to stay calm while preparing for landing. But I didn't have enough time. I landed headfirst on top of a polgueira tree. Instantly, I felt excruciate pain in my spine, the back of my head, elbows, and leg. A sharp, dead branch penetrated deep into my left leg.

With the branch still pierced into my leg, I carefully lowered myself to the ground. I sat on the ground and tried removing the branch, but I couldn't stop shaking. I took a few short breaths. Frightened, I tried again, but the pain was too intense. *Okay, Clesio, on three.* One. Two. Three. Four. I gathered my courage, and I pulled it as hard as I could. But it only came about a half way out. The pain felt as if someone was forcing a hot metal through my leg. I gathered my courage once more, and howling, I yanked the branch off. The blood instantly began spraying, so I promptly tore my shirt to wrap around the wound. Limping, I collected as much plants as I could and tramped home.

Besides taking care of the animals, Bety would force Nelson and me to work in the farm without food because we would leave so early in the morning, before food was ready. It didn't matter if it was too hot or a full day's labor or even storming. In addition to our land near the house, we owned five acres about an hour away, where we frequently farmed. Getting there was like hiking up a mountain. I hated this field because the trip to and from it was exhausting. Halfway there, I would be out of breath, my legs would begin to shake, and I could feel my muscles burning. Even though we hadn't been able to bring food, no one would make this trek to feed us.

One time, Nelson and I were sent to dig holes to plant seeds. During the dry season, we couldn't find anything to eat in the field unlike during the green season. After working half a day, we were famished and thirsty.

"Clesio, I don't think we can finish digging today. I'm thirsty," Nelson claimed. I paused digging and looked at him. He was covered with dust and sweat. His eyes revealed his exhaustion.

"We have to. If we go home now, Bety will force us to come back here. We both know how torturous that is."

"It's almost 2:00 p.m., and no one has even cared enough to bring us food and water. What does she expect?"

"She expects us to finish digging, no matter what. Isn't that obvious?"

He grabbed his digging hoe and smashed it against the ground.

"This is bullshit. I'm going to dig until 3:00 p.m., and then I am leaving. If you want to stay, then stay! You are more than welcome to stay. But I'm done with this bullshit. We are working like slaves, but no one and I mean no one has the heart to at least feed us. Look around. We are the only ones working in this heat. It's over a hundred degrees, and it feels like two hundred. I'm thirsty, sweaty, hungry, and tried, so at exactly three o'clock, I'm out of here . . ."

"Hell no, I'm not staying here by myself. If you go, I'm going with you. But I will be surprised if Bety doesn't force us to return."

He picked up his hoe and resumed digging.

"I don't care. I'm still leaving."

"Okay, I will be right after you."

At 3:00 p.m., we left, and upon our arrival home, we could see Bety, Aunt Eloisa, and two neighbors playing cards for candy outside. From the distance, I could hear Eloisa's loud voice, arguing about the rules.

"I guess now we know why no one brought us food," I said, shaking my head.

"What did you expect? Did you really believe they didn't bring us food because they were working?" Nelson asked.

"Oh no, I could never think that," I answered low so they wouldn't hear.

Bety got up and strode toward us as soon as she saw us. Nelson and I looked at each other, and we shook our heads, anticipating that something bad was about to happen.

"What are you guys doing here?" Bety asked, pointing her finger toward the field, indicating that we had to go back.

"We were starving that's why we came to eat." I glowered as I sat down on top of the water tank near the kitchen.

"Well, there isn't any food here, and the farm work needs to done today."

"We are tired and hungry, so we will finish it tomorrow morning," I pleaded. She stomped closer to me.

"No, Clesio, Nooo! Today, I said. What part of today don't you understand?"

"Bety, it's your turn. Are you still playing or what?" Eloisa nudged her.

"Yes, I'm coming. Guys, that field must be done today." She then returned to her card game.

Despair and anger built in my body as I imagined climbing back to the field in the humidity. Nelson grabbed his hoe and marched forward.

"Clesio, let's go!" Nelson shouted angrily. I could hear the frustration in his voice.

"I'm not going," I grumbled, hesitating. Bety immediately rose and headed toward me, tight-lipped.

"Where is my electric cord?"

"Nelson, wait for me, I'm coming!" I screamed, running toward the field.

"Oh, I thought you weren't coming," Nelson mocked me, smiling.

"Nelson, not now. Don't make this more painful than it already is."

Nelson and I struggled the whole way, barely had the energy to take steps. Utilizing branches of trees and plants known as carapate to haul ourselves up, we forced our weak legs to work. Carapate has strong leaves about forty inches long, which extend nearly the pathway, making them the perfect tool for climbing the steep hill.

An hour and a half later, we arrived at the field, out of breath. I dropped to the ground and lay there for about ten minutes. While lying there, I thought about how unfair and painful my life had been.

"Come on, dude, we have to finish so we can go home," Nelson pleaded.

"What is the use? What is the point of going home? Going home to what?"

CHAPTER 9

Aunt Eloisa: Evildoer

Across the street from us lived my aunt Eloisa with her two daughters, Jacira and Jandira, and her son, Jelson. Although they owned the house across the street from my grandmother's house, they spent the majority of their time with us. They ate there, showered there, and slept there. In other words, we were nine people living at my grandmother's house.

Eloisa was in her thirties, heavy, and tall. She had long black hair, which she often covered with a piece of old clothing. Her round face and black eyes made her look frightening. No one in the neighborhood ever messed with her because her evil appearance scared them. She also behaved like a man—at home she always wore large jeans and shirts. Growing up, she spent the majority of her life surrounded by men. She would play soccer, drink alcohol, party, and sometimes fight with them.

Eloisa served in the Cape Verde local militia, where she was responsible for maintaining order in the community. When riots occurred, she would march into the middle of the crowds to break them up. As a result, she became even more aggressive. Every time she came near me, I would grow uncomfortable. Although she wasn't the guardian of Nelson, Neminha, and me, she always forced us to perform her commands as well as Bety's.

Eloisa was too indulgent with her children, who always seemed to get away with everything. They didn't even need a permission to do or go anywhere. The same wasn't true for my sister, brother, and me. We weren't even permitted go to our next-door neighbor's without permission. We couldn't have fun like her children or even like the other children in the neighborhood. In order for us to get permission, we had to work on the farm all day or successfully complete both aunts' tasks. Eloisa's children, on the other hand, were never assigned any hard work, such as farm chores.

In addition, if my siblings and I made a minor mistake, Eloisa would beat us with anything she had in her hands, mostly a hateful electric cord. However, her children could smash furniture against the ground or steal items and still not be punished. Also, when she ordered us to perform tasks, we had to promptly fulfill her requests, without complaint; otherwise she would slice us. While everyone else feared Eloisa, her own children disobeyed her. Ironically, this didn't bother Eloisa. Many times she would send Jacira or Jelson to perform a task, and if they refused to comply, instead of disciplining them, Eloisa would immediately demand one of us to do it.

Jelson quickly learned that he had great leverage over me, the power to get me in trouble anytime he wished. How? Simple. He could just invent any lie and tell Bety or his mother, and I was toast. He would have me do all his chores, like cleaning his bicycle and washing his sneakers, or would even confiscate all my food. To avoid being beaten, I would obey.

Besides treating us unequally, Eloisa used Nelson and me as beasts of burden. Because Eloisa constantly physically and emotionally abused us, we were too vulnerable to resist her. One time, Eloisa decided to build small guest quarters next to her house; instead of hiring a truck driver to deliver her materials, she forced Nelson and me to walk to the beach, approximately four miles away, to gather and bring sand home to make cement. The filled sandbags were huge, and the steepness of the path was treacherous. One minor shift of weight and the bag could roll us to the bottom. Even empty-handed people would struggle to walk the path. Every day, Nelson and I were sent for the sand, we knew there was a high possibility we might not return. The path was in the middle of nowhere; therefore, screaming would be pointless. We recognized the need to create an emergency plan.

"If you fall, I will do my best to carry you home, but if I fall, just check if I'm okay, and then go call for help," eighteen-year-old Nelson said with tears in his eyes.

His remarks touched me deeply; it felt like my heart and spirit were crushed. As he spoke, my steps became heavier and heavier as if someone had added weights to my shoulders. I, too, felt like crying, but I didn't want to show him weakness. I put on a straight face and looked at him.

"Don't you dare talk like that. We will be fine," I said firmly but doubtful.

He stopped, turned, and walked to me.

"I know, but just in case something happens, we will know what to do."

I fought the urge to cry.

"There is nothing to be ready for. Nothing is going to happen to us," I responded, poking his chest with my finger.

"I'm only making sure we are prepared."

"Prepared for what? I don't want to think about it." I walked past him. "Clesio, stop!"

I paused and then turned slowly. "What?"

"Why are you getting mad?"

"I'm not mad." There was an awkward silence. "I don't know what I am feeling. It's just not fair. They are home having fun, while we are talking about the possibility of dying."

He wiped away his tears. "I know it isn't fair. They don't even care about us. But we have to stay strong."

"It hurts, knowing that no one cares about us," I said, rubbing my eyes. Nelson inched toward me.

"No one may care about us, but we care about each other, and that's what matters."

I smiled, feeling like someone had lifted a boulder from my heart. Nelson's smile was so wide, it made wrinkles on his forehead.

"Yeah, you're right. As long as we have each other, we don't need anybody."

"That's the spirit." We walked toward the beach, with me leading the way.

"Clesio?" Nelson called softly.

I turned around.

"Yes? I'm not going to fall," I said sarcastically, laughing.

"I didn't say anything about falling." He laughed. "What is the first thing you will do when we go to the United States?"

"Eat lots of food."

"Eat food, seriously?"

"I'm always hungry." We laughed.

"Seriously, what will you do?" I paused for a moment to think about which of the million things I would do first.

"Reenroll in school."

He gave me a thumbs-up, indicating that he liked the idea.

"What do you want to go to school for?"

"I don't know yet."

"You should study mathematics since you are good in math."

"I'll think about it. Besides I have enough time. What about you?"

"I'm going to create a studio so I can record my own songs," said Nelson with excitement. I noticed his face glowing as he spoke.

"That's great. I can sing with you—well, scream with you."

"Clesio, Clesio, be careful," he alerted me.

I instantly stopped.

"What happened?"

"Watch your steps because this downhill stretch is extremely dangerous. Some rocks are loose, so if you don't walk carefully, you may slip and roll all the way down." He directed me to walk behind him in case, I slipped, he could catch me. My legs began to shake slightly.

"Thanks. Now I am scared."

"There is nothing to be scared about. Just watch your step."

"Okay Jesus," I said, smiling. "You do realize it's going to be ten times harder to climb this hill with heavy sand?"

"I thought you said we were going to be fine. Where is your positive spirit?"

"Oh yeah, right. We are. We are going to be fine."

We struggled our way home and made four or five more trips. By our last, it was nearly dark outside, and we were so tired that we decided to stay home to rest. We were too exhausted even to eat. Nevertheless, when Eloisa discovered us, she promptly started toward us, and from the distance I could hear her anger voice. She demanded we return for more sand. Devastated and hopeless, we turned around to bring more sand. On the way back, we could barely shift the heavy bags on our shoulders.

"I can't go any farther," I said, breathing heavily as I climbed the deep hill with the heavy sand on top of my head. The sand probably weighed about ninety pound, but it felt heavier with my weak muscles. I dropped my bag a half way up. Nelson looked at me, drained, and then dropped his.

"Walking up this steep hill with this stupid sand is torture," Nelson stated, as he threw himself abruptly on top of hay. I sat next to him, still breathing heavily. "One day Eloisa will pay for this abuse."

"That's for sure," I replied as Nelson's head dropped. "I'm exhausted, and look at my legs. They are shaking. I can even feel my muscles stretching, and I can barely move. But despite all these, you know what hurts me the most?"

"What?"

"The fact that Eloisa only does this to us. She never forces her children to do anything. It's her sand. Why are we the ones to risk our lives for it?"

Nelson craned his head and looked at me. His eyes were watery. "I wish we had a better life," he said softy.

"Me too. I agree with you that as long as we have each other we don't need anybody else, but sometimes I wish someone else cared about me, too," I said, rubbing the heel of my palm against my chest. "My life has been a nightmare ever since I was five years old," I added.

Nelson reached and hugged me. "I care about you, and nothing will change that," he comforted me.

"I just want a normal life, you know. A life where people would care about me and treat me like a human being. A life free from abuse. I want to go to bed without having to worry about my tomorrow. I don't want to fear that I may not come back home when I leave in the morning."

"Things will get better when we go to the United States. People will care about us and treat us better there."

"Yeah, if we are still alive by then."

"Come on, Clesio, what can possibly happen to us?"

"Nelson, I have been living this depressing life for a long time. Many times, I ask myself if this life is worth living. Look down there." I pointed down the hill. "We are risking our lives every time we come here. If we slip down this hill, there is no chance of surviving!"

"Neither of us is going to fall. We just need to be careful. We have to stay positive."

"Anyways, we have to keep moving before it gets too dark."

After a ten-minute rest, I helped my brother lift his sand onto his back, and while carrying it, he attempted to help me lift mine. But his foot slipped, and his sand bag knocked him forward, and they both started rolling down the hill. When I immediately dropped my bag to help my brother, it also rolled down the hill. As Nelson was rolling, he managed to grab onto a plant, and with my weak muscles, I crept toward him and helped him get back to his feet. I paused and watched the bags rolling, imagining how painful it would be if they were our bodies smashing against the rock. Fighting not to cry, we crawled back down the hill for our bags because we knew if we arrived home without them, Eloisa would beat us.

It wasn't until eleven at night that we arrived home. While my brother and I had been struggling carrying sand, Eloisa, her children, and Bety were at home playing cards for candy. When we arrived, they didn't look up from their cards to find out why we took so long to arrive. Eloisa didn't even say thank-you. Angry and frustrated, we didn't eat dinner. Actually, Nelson didn't eat dinner. I did.

At six the next morning, Eloisa woke Nelson and me to go to *monda*.

"Nelson! Clesio! Wake up," Eloisa demanded. I lay there, pretending to be asleep. "Do you guys want me get cold water, or will you get up on your own?" Nelson got up. Then Eloisa walked to my side of the bed and shook me. "Get up!"

"What?" I asked, annoyed. She removed my blanket. Anger built up in my body.

"You guys have to go Monda." She pointed outside, indicating we needed to move now.

"I have a headache from carrying the sand yesterday!" I raised my voice, which caused my head to hurt even more. She laughed sarcastically as though I was lying.

"Nice try. Get up now!"

"I'm serious. I have a headache."

"Well, too bad. You still have to go."

Nelson looked at me and then at Eloisa. "He doesn't have to. I will go by myself."

"Shut your mouth, Nelson!" she shouted at him. She placed her forefinger across her lips, signaling Nelson to keep quiet. As I tried getting up, I felt pain all over my body, still sore from the night before. I could hardly move because my legs, back, arms, and head were throbbing. The brightness of the sunlight reflected in my eyes, adding to my headache. Nelson was also in pain and was having trouble walking. I wanted to tell Eloisa off, but I knew it would only cause more harm. So I forced myself and went to Monda.

By the time we arrived at the field, the sun had risen, and it was already very hot. The hotter it got, the worse my headache became.

"Are you okay?" Nelson asked, worried.

"Yeah, I'm fine." I masked my pain.

"You don't look fine to me."

"Fine, my body and head hurt, but there is nothing we can do about it."

Nelson stopped and looked around. He spotted a shadow under a tree. "Go lie down under that tree right there."

"We both know I can't do that. If we don't do what we're supposed to, Eloisa will beat both of us, and I can't afford to be beaten in this condition."

"I will work fast so I can cover your share as well."

"Are you sure? I can see you are also in pain."

"I'm fine. We have to help each other. As you can see, no one else cares about us, so in order for us to survive, we must be there for each other. Go lie down and cool yourself. That will help your headache."

"Okay, thank you."

Trying to cover as much field as possible, Nelson forced himself to work through pain and exhaustion, without taking a break, only to find out it wasn't enough. From the distance, Nelson saw Eloisa appear with food on top of her head. He quickly alerted me, and I promptly grabbed my garden hoe and started to work. When Eloisa arrived, she stood approximately five feet away from us with a disappointed look.

"What were you doing that you guys did so little?" Eloisa asked.

"It is my fau—"

She interrupted me.

"You guys have no idea who you are playing with!" She immediately turned around and left with our lunch. I picked my hoe and smashed it against the ground.

"I'm done. I can't take this bullshit anymore! This is her field, and we aren't obligated to work for her. I have a terrible headache, my muscles are burning, and now I have to work hungry!" I said as I punched a tree as hard as I could. "And now my hand." I dropped my knees to the ground, pulling my hair in frustration, and burst into tears. Nelson walked up to me, and from bended knees, he hugged me.

"I'm so sorry."

"I want to scream, I want to scream."

"Go ahead, scream," Nelson encouraged me, crying.

"I can't. My headache will get worse."

"Do you want to go home?"

"No . . . I want to die."

These abuses occurred repeatedly, and sometimes my sister Neminha would also be a victim.

A year later, after Nelson and I had worked on the farm every day from eight to six, Eloisa sent Neminha, Nelson, and me to a field about a mile away to gather and bring peanut plants to a storage shed near the house. The peanuts had already been harvested, leaving only the vines. Vines are the most difficult and frustrating plants to transport because when they are tied together, they will easily break apart.

Although it was nearly dark, we set off to fulfill Eloisa's request. After gathering vines, we tied them together into a huge ball. As we carried them, the bundles kept breaking apart, which really slowed our process. My sister was so frustrated that she cried for the duration of the trip.

Upon our arrival home, we found Eloisa holding the electric cord in her hands, and without inquiring about the reason for our delay, she began hitting us. Then she sent us back to bring more peanut plants. At this point, it was so dark that we couldn't even see our steps.

We crawled back to the field for more peanut plants.

"Neminha, don't even bother crying. It's not going to heal this pain," I said, holding onto Nelson.

"Clesio, I'm not in the mood to talk!" I stopped to wait for her.

"Hold on to me." She grabbed my shirt from behind as I grabbed Nelson's, and Nelson navigated the way.

We blindly braced ourselves against the wall as a guideline and crawled or stepped into air as we headed toward the field. Forty minutes later, we arrived at the field.

"How are we going to tie the vines in the dark? I can't even see where they are." Nelson worried.

"Let's do them one at a time, so we can help each other," I suggested as I bumped into a tree.

"Are you okay?" Nelson asked.

"I'm fine. Neminha, enough crying," I said, annoyed.

"Clesio, please don't make me take this anger out on you!" I walked up to her and hugged her.

"Listen, I'm not trying to piss you off. I'm sorry if I did. We just need to stay strong. Yes, I know what we are going through is painful, but we can't let anyone step on us or get to us because one day we will succeed. We can't afford to show weaknesses. Me, you, and Nelson, together, we are stronger than Eloisa and Bety combined."

"Thank you, Clesio. I really needed to hear that." I wiped tears away from her face.

We struggled to bring the vines home, stumbling the entire way. Upon our arrival home, we noticed Eloisa waiting for us on the porch.

"Guys, stay strong. Don't show her that we are scared," I advised Nelson and Neminha.

"Where have you guys been?" Eloisa asked, furious. "You guys were gone for three hours. What could possibly cause you to take this long?"

I dropped my vines and took a step toward her. "That was the question you should have asked before you sliced us with the stupid cord!" I raised my voice with a straight face.

"Are you trying to get smart with me?"

"Not at all. I just find it fascinating that you beat us and sent us back in the dark without finding the true reason for our delay and only now you are interested." I walked past her. She grabbed my hand and pulled me toward her.

"Listen, you fool!"

"What? Are you going to beat me again? Go ahead. Make it quick." She looked at me, shook her head, and pushed me away. Her dark face turned red.

"Get out of my face before I kill you."

Neminha immediately grabbed my hand and pulled me into the room. "What got into you just now?" Neminha asked, amazed.

"I'm tired just of being treated like a slave."

CHAPTER 10

Life in High School

If the trip to middle school every day had been exhausting, at least it wasn't life threatening. I went to high school in São Filipe, which is about an hour and a half away from São Jorge. Families couldn't afford to pay for private transportation to attend school each day, and because the government had to provide transportations to all cities, only one construction truck was available for each city to transport students to and from school. Yes, students had to ride in the back of a construction truck. The combination of open back and hazardous road conditions made for great danger on our journey to school. Those construction trucks had no seats, so we all had to stand. There was a metal chain across the back, dividing the truck bed into two parts. The students on both sides of the chain would hold on for dear life.

There was an average of sixty students in the truck, making traveling on the narrow road extremely dangerous. The road was built from bricks without paving and had bumps everywhere, causing the truck to bounce continuously throughout the journey. Furthermore, the road was only as wide as a truck, yet it was used for both directions of traffic. Most of the time, when we had oncoming traffic, the driver had to back up until he found a wider space to allow the cars to pass. The road had a lot of curves, which made it very difficult to see oncoming cars. Also, along the road were several curves on the edge of cliffs. Thus, the truck driver had to drive at the right speed because otherwise it would veer off those edges. Ninety percent of the time, drivers would either speed on the curves or drive entirely in the middle of the road, instead of driving on one side to prevent collisions. When the driver turned widely, some students would almost fall off, and sometimes we had to hold on to each other to prevent falling out of the truck. In addition, every time the driver suddenly stepped on the brake, we all would fall on top of each other.

One day, the driver stopped suddenly, and several students fell on me. The force pressed my back against the chain and almost split me in half. I could feel the metal digging into my waist as the students fell on top of me. I tried to turn on top my stomach to relieve the pressure, but the sharp metal tore into my skin even more. They pressed down into me, trying to get back to their own feet, and I prayed to stay in one piece. When I got back to my feet, I had no idea of my whereabouts, and I could hardly breathe. Everything was black and blurry for about twenty minutes. I heard some students screaming while others were crying, but the voices sounded as though they were coming from far away. One student noticed I was in danger of falling off the truck. He brought me to a safer corner and held me for the remaining of the trip.

Another factor contributing to the perilous ride was the lack of streetlights. Because there were more students than the capacity of the truck allowed, the driver had to make two trips. As a result, the first-trip students had to leave home at four thirty in the morning so the second-trip students would make school on time. However, at the time, it would still be dark, so if an object was on the road or if an animal crossed it, the driver wouldn't be able to see it in time to stop safely. Several times, indeed, we would encounter goats, cows, chickens, and other animals crossing the road, requiring the driver to hit the brakes. One morning, a black cat was crossing the road, and the driver didn't see it until he was right on top of it. The driver tried his best to stop the truck safely, but there wasn't enough time. So he pressed hard the on brake, causing one student to nearly fall off the truck.

Returning from school on the truck was even more challenging because I would be starved, exhausted, irritated, and sometimes suffering from a terrible headache. I could barely stand on my legs. Therefore, traveling in a crowded, bouncing construction truck where students would fall on top of me was terrifying.

Besides risking my life on the truck, I had to starve every day. My father once sent me money to buy food at school, but Bety confiscated all of it. Consequently, I had to stay hungry all day. I would have my last meal at 9:00 p.m. and wait until 4:00 p.m. the next day to have my first meal. Because I was one of the first-trip students, I didn't have enough time to get ready and make breakfast. Making anything took a great deal of time since we didn't have a stove. In order to make breakfast, I had to build the fire, which alone would take twenty minutes to a half hour. In addition, the burnt wood would produce smoke and ashes that would transfer to my clothes. Therefore, if I decided to make breakfast, I couldn't wash up for school until I finished eating.

Many of the students would have money to buy snacks between classes, but not me. In Cape Verde, students didn't like to share, or even if they did, they wouldn't have enough to share, and there was no school program or any charity in place to provide free food. So while at school, I didn't have access to food of any kind. All I could do was watch other students eat, while my stomach growled, feeling as though my intestines were sticking together. It felt as if something was eating my intestines and stomach. I suffered from a hunger headache almost every day, which contributed to my poor academic performance. Also, I experienced dizziness many times, and sometimes I even had to hold on to something to prevent from collapsing.

Several times Bety would fail to provide us dinner, or if she did, it would be only water with sugar and three cookies. She would feed only her son and herself. Many times, I had to sleep hungry and stay hungry all day until I arrived home at four or five o'clock. Often, I would faint and suffer from double vision, stomachache, and light-headedness from hunger.

One day everything was split in half—people had two heads, and the ground's surface appeared deeper than it really was. As I was walking into class, I fell, and all I could remember was waking up surrounded by several students and professors.

"What happened?" I asked, confused. Everything was blurred. I reached for my forehead, and I felt warm liquid. I panicked.

"You fell down," a student replied.

"I think I'm bleeding," I said as I attempted to get up.

"Stop, stop, don't get up yet," my professor cautioned me while pressing my shoulders down.

What's going on?

I could hear people scream. "Get some water! Go get water!"

"What did you eat today?" my professor asked.

"Nothing."

"You haven't eaten anything today?"

"No," I answered softly.

My professor's eyes widened, and he shook his head.

"You haven't eaten yet, and it's almost two o'clock?" he restated, surprised. "What time do you normally eat?" He helped me to raise my upper body so I could sit.

"I eat when I get home around 4:00 p.m." My head dropped. A student arrived with a bottle of water and handed it to my professor.

"So you come to school without a breakfast and have to wait until you get home to eat?" My professor asked, shocked. I nodded. "Drink some water. Why don't you buy food?" he asked as he cleared the blood from my face.

"Because I don't have any money." He shook his head in disbelief. I noticed my knees, hands, and head were shaking.

"That's why you passed out. Your body doesn't have enough nutrition to function."

"Yeah, I didn't even eat dinner last night."

"It's about class time, but I will dismiss class early, and I will take you to eat at a restaurant nearby." I nodded, accepting the offer. He helped me get to my feet and walk to class.

After class, my professor and I walked to a restaurant about five minutes from the school.

"Thank you for buying me food. I very much appreciate it."

"You're welcome. Where are you from?"

"São Jorge."

"Oh, you're one of 4:30 a.m. students?"

"Yes."

The waitress handed us the menu. I was nervous, scared, and surprised because it was my first time ever in a restaurant.

"You can order anything you like," he encouraged me. I ordered the lunch special, which included rice, shrimp, and beans.

Later he asked, "How is your food?"

"Really good. This is the best food I ever ate." I smiled.

My professor smiled back. "I'm glad you like it." I could tell he had a lot of questions, but he decided to only ask the basic ones since he didn't know me very well.

"Are you okay there?" he asked to break the silence.

"Yes, I'm full already."

"If you want, you can take the rest with you."

"No, it's okay. It's impossible to bring food back in the truck."

"Yes, that's right, silly me," he said, smiling.

Although Bety knew I would spend all day at school without eating, she wouldn't save me any food when I came home, or if she did, it would be just plain rice. In addition to the money for my care, my father sent money for groceries, but Bety, instead, spent it on herself. Many times there wouldn't be any food for my brother, sister, and me. During the green season, when I came from school starving, I would be able to look for potatoes and fruits in the fields. During the dry season, though, I would remain famished. When we had food—such as meat, green beans, and rice—my sister would save some for me, but Bety and her son would eat all the meat and beans. If there was any plain rice left, Bety would set aside a plate, and by the time I arrived home, it would be cold and dry.

One day, I came home from school starving, and I went straight to the kitchen, only to find a plate with dry white rice. I held the plate in my hand, looked at it for a few seconds, and shook my head in disbelief. *This sucks. It's so unfair.* Because there was no another alternative, I had to eat the nasty-looking rice. It tasted like hard plastic. It was so dry that it wouldn't pass through my throat, even though I was starving. I decided to add a tablespoon of oil to help me swallow. Big mistake. The oil sank and stayed at the bottom of my plate. As I was about to finish eating, Eloisa saw the oil on my plate, smiled, and walked way. *That's not a good sign.*

About two hours later, Eloisa told Bety that I had put oil on my food. Bety instantly sent Nelson to call me from Eloisa's house. As I was arriving home, I observed that Bety had the electric cord in her hands. It was humid, so I wasn't wearing a shirt. *Why does she have the cord? Wait, did I do something wrong? I can't remember doing anything wrong. Maybe she just has it for something else?* I hoped I was right. When I was a yard away from the house, she advanced toward me, swinging the cord back and forth. *Oh crap, I guess it's for me. Oh my God, I don't even have a shirt on.* My heart palpitated as I got closer. My steps felt heavier as blood rushed to my heart. I unconsciously began rubbing my sweaty hands against each other. Standing with one arm holding my other elbow, I prayed for my life.

Without any explanation, she began hitting me with the cord.

"Can you at least tell me why you are hitting me?" I yelled. Eloisa was sitting about ten feet away from us, smiling. Nelson's head dropped, while Neminha went inside, crying.

"Oh, you don't know? Here is something to help you remember," Bety argued, as she swung the cord. I crossed my arms on my chest, and I allowed her to hit me until she was satisfied. I was so angry that I didn't cry. Not even a single tear came out of my eyes.

After she sliced my entire back, she stopped.

"Are you done?" I asked with a straight face. She looked at me, shook her head, and walked away.

"Let me leave you before I kill you," she replied, glowering.

"Is it possible to know why I have been sliced?" I asked furious.

She turned around. Her eyes widened, irritated. I inched toward her and looked into her eyes, waiting for an answer.

"For pouring oil on your food!" she snapped.

"Really? For oil? For the oil you bought with my own father's money? Wow, that's nice to know," I said sarcastically, fighting the urge to cry. Her face turned as red as my back. She looked stupid and guilty. I sat down on a concrete bench, and Nelson and Neminha sat beside me, Nelson on my left and Neminha on my right. "Hi, kids," I said as I wasn't in pain.

"Clesio, you aren't human. You aren't even crying," Nelson said, amazed. I looked at him and threw him a fake smile over my shoulder.

"Shut up, Nelson!" Neminha shouted. "This isn't a joking matter."

"Why not? It has already happened, and there's nothing we can do about it now, so we might as well have fun with it." I continued fighting not to cry.

"I guess you aren't human," Neminha answered, smiling. As I sat there, I could feel blood rolling down my back. I reached for my back, and my hand was covered in blood. Still setting, I played with my bloody hand.

"Are you okay?" Neminha asked, as she wiped tears from her eyes.

"Yes, I'm fine," I pretended. "I have never felt better."

I moved slightly, and I felt blood dripping from my back. Neminha took a warm cloth, gently trying to clean up the wounds. I bit the inside of my lip, trying to keep the tears at bay. The warm water felt nice against my hot back, but the skin pulled with the cloth, and that was almost worse than the beating.

Though I attempted to be strong, I collapsed a few hours later because I had lost so much blood. I became woozy, and my steps felt heavy as I felt my frigid body shaking, even though it was nearly eighty degrees. My back felt as if it was on fire, and for a couple of weeks, I couldn't sleep on it. I would only sleep shirtless, without covering myself, because my clothes and sheets would stick to my wounds.

It took nearly a year for the wounds to heal because there was no medical care available nearby. Also as they were healing, either Eloisa or Bety would hit me again, causing them to bleed all over again.

Chapter 11

The Beauty of Salina: So Close, So Far

São Jorge on the island of Fogo is well-known for Salina Beach. It has pristine azure water, shining black volcanic sand, and a breathtaking natural stone arch about 150 feet tall, from which people can dive and do back flips. Salina is the perfect beach for people to cool down during hot weather. Its exquisite beauty attracts both locals and tourists from all over the world. It certainly lured me as a fifteen-year-old.

A trip to Salina Beach invited fun. The most popular game was diving about thirty feet to the ebony bottom to hide an object such, as small shiny can. People would create two teams, usually of about four people on each side. One team would dive and hide something, after which the other would dive and search. Reaching the bottom took about a minute and required tremendous intake of breath. The breath would be held on the descent and during the hiding for as long as possible, then would be slowly exhaled on the way up. The round-trip could take as long as five minutes. Once the hiding team reached the surface, the searcher would dive for a predetermined time. If the searchers couldn't locate and return with the object within seven minutes, the point would go to the other team. Then the team would switch roles.

Although I liked both roles, searching was my favorite because it required teamwork. While searching, we had to constantly look at our teammates for signals. If someone found the object, he would give a thumbs-up, indicating he had located it.

One time, it was my team's turn to search. Anxiously waiting for the hiding person to return, I could feel the warm sun on my back, the drying water on my body. As the water evaporated from my face, arms, back, stomach, and legs, it turned into salt. I wiped salt from my face and tasted. *Not bad. This is delicious.* After he returned, our team took our position, and I stood on an edge of the arch so I could gain speed on the dive.

A few minutes later, one person from the opposite team began to count down. "Three . . . two . . ." I inhaled my breath. "One . . . go!" I jumped.

As I dove, I could see tiny shining fish swimming near me. Halfway down, I felt the necessity to breathe. My lungs wanted to expand. I fought the urge, trying to hold my breath for as long as I could so I would be able to stay longer to find the can.

At the bottom, I grabbed a rock of about twenty pounds to hold me down so I could look for disturbed rocks, sand, or holes. Then I felt little fish nipping at me. *Come on, fish. Now isn't a good time to play.*

I released the rock and began searching under nearby rocks. *It must be under these rocks.* But it wasn't there. I looked at my teammates, then at my watch, and I had a minute and a half to retrieve the object out of the water in order to score. *Or maybe it is in those holes over there.* I swam toward the holes, sticking my hand into one covered with algae. I could feel something soft and slippery, so I grabbed it. *What's this weird feeling?* I pulled my hand out, and it was a jellyfish. All the members of my team had already left. I looked at my watch and saw I had only one minute and ten seconds left. *Okay, Clesio, you have to go to now.*

As I was leaving, I saw a bright reflection. *Could it be the object?* I looked down. It appeared to be what I was seeking. My eyes began to hurt as I struggled to hold my breath. I turned around, dove down, and grabbed the can. *Yes, baby, this is what I'm talking about.* I looked at the watch, forty seconds left, less than the time it required to raise the can out of the water to show the other team. To break to the surface within the remaining time, I pressed my feet against the bottom as hard as I could, propelled myself up, and slowly began to exhale.

When I was just under the surface, I immediately raised the hand holding the can out of the water. Even opponents were amazed with my performance. My teammates jumped into the water and raised me up, throwing me around.

"That was an incredible job, Clesio! We are so proud of you," one member of the team said.

"Thank you," I said with a smile.

A second popular game was back flip. People would climb up on the bridge and jump. The bridge has layers, creating a ladder from the bottom to the top. Its rocks are sharpl, with arches. The bridge is tall enough for people to perform as many as eight to ten flips. Even kids as young as five would perform back flips and dive from the bridge.

At the beginning, I was afraid even to go near the stone bridge because people would push me into the water. But when I saw five-year-olds having fun doing back flips, I decided to learn to jump. I began from the lowest crag and worked my way up. With every jump, I moved a little higher.

Come on. If you jumped from that height, you can jump from this one. There's only a tiny difference.

Half way to the top, I stood on an edge and slowly leaned over to measure the deepness. *Oh my God, that's deep. You can do this, Clesio. It's only a tiny difference.* I jumped. *This is awesome . . .* Three jumps after the halfway mark, the height was about 125 feet.

Standing near the edge, I could see a lot of people in the water and on the bridge, jumping. *Come on, Clesio, it's only a tiny difference.* Bouncing on my tiptoe, I gathered my courage while trying to stop my legs from shaking. *Oh, maybe if I come running, I can just jump off without thinking about it.*

Okay, on three. One . . . two . . . three . . .

I ran toward the edge at full speed but lost my courage and balance right before reaching the edge. I waved my arms and dragged my feet against the rocks, trying to stop. Just when I was about to fall, I regained my balance.

"What's the problem? Are you scared?" I turned my head to see my friend Jailson behind me.

"Nooooo."

"Of course not. You don't look scared at all."

"Okay, you got me, but today is my first time, and I'm more than a half way through working my way to the top."

"You are doing it all wrong, you know."

"What do you mean?"

"You have to add some fun into it."

"And what do you suggest?"

"See, I don't tell. I show." He smiled.

"Then show me." Knowing Jailson, I realized I had just set myself up for a big challenge.

"Oh no, man, you have to be ready for this," he said, nodding.

"Come on, man, I was born ready."

"Are you sure? Because when you agree, there is no going back." *It can't be that bad.*

"I'm all for it," I fibbed.

He looked at me, laughing. I could tell he was excited about my decision.

"Where is your brother?"

My eyes widened.

"I don't need permission from my brother, you know."

He shook his head, laughing. "You are silly. I'm not seeking for his permission. I need an assistant, and your brother is good at it."

My brother is involved? I was wrong. It can be that bad.

"He's swimming over there." Jailson called my brother and took him aside. My brother kept nodding as my friend whispered in his ear. Then they returned, laughing.

"Okay, Nelson, go in front of Clesio, and I will go behind him."

"I don't know what you guys are up to, but I have a bad feeling about this."

"Clesio, you have no right to talk anymore. Just follow Nelson." Nelson led the way to the bridge.

"Oh no, I'm not jumping off the bridge!" My legs began to shake. My brother grabbed my right hand firmly while my friend grabbed my left. My friend looked at me and winked.

"Who said anything about jumping? We are just crossing the bridge because I'm going to show you something fun on the other side."

They grabbed my hands tighter and tighter as we approached the bridge. Once on the top, they ran off and released me into the air.

"Now you are on your own!" they yelled, releasing me before we hit the water.

My heart dropped, and I could not feel any part of my body. *I'm going to die. That's it. I'm going to die.* I closed my eyes and crossed my arms over my chest as I broke the water's surface.

"That was awesome!" I yelled when I returned to the surface.

After the games, Nelson, our friends Jailson and Romario, our cousins Steven and Adilson, and I would usually go fish to eat. We would bring fishing supplies, wood, hay, and sometimes a sheet of metal so we could cook the fish. We discovered a hole about five feet wide nearby where we could store our knife, matches, and petroleum prior to swimming. At the hole, we built a grill by collecting four rocks, placing them in a square, and laying the metal sheet on top of them. We then layered the wood, using the hay as tinder and the petroleum for accelerant. As soon as the fire was burning, we carefully lined the fish on the grill.

"What time are we going fishing today?" Jailson asked, looking at his watch, indicating that we should go now.

"Soon," Steven replied.

"I have an idea this time," Jailson said as he squeezed between Steven and me.

"Oh no, not again, Jailson. The last time you had an idea, you almost gave me a heart attack."

"Are you dead?"

"Well, I'm not sure . . ."

"Clesio, you will be fine. Jailson, what is your idea?" Nelson asked.

"Since we have to fish to eat, I suggest we make it fun." *Here we go with fun again*. Everyone looked at Jailson, waiting for him to finish.

"Go on . . .," Steven nudged.

"Let's form teams and compete against each other."

Steven instantly leaned and hugged Jailson.

"That's a great idea, Jailson. You're a genius," he said.

"I know, I know . . .," Jailson said, smiling.

"The team that catches the most fish will do an easy task, like turning the fish on the grill, while the team that catches the least will do the tedious tasks, like skin the fish and light the fire," Steven suggested, excited.

"How are we going to make teams with five people? Romario isn't here today. One team will have one person more than the other, and that's not fair," Adilson worried.

"What about if we make two teams of two, and one person will be assistant for both teams?" I suggested. They nodded. "The person will be responsible for preparing our fishing supplies, like adding worms to the hook. And of course, he will be guaranteed fish and automatically be excluded from any task, and all he has to do is ea—"

"Call me an assistant," Steven interrupted. "I will be the assistant."

"Okay, let's make teams now," Jailson urged. "Clesio and Nelson, Adilson and I.'

"Oh no, I need to get my revenge on you and Nelson. You team with Nelson so I get both of you in one round."

"Okay, as you please," Jailson agreed. "Let's go, let's go."

We rushed to our favorite fishing area, two minutes past the stone bridge. The area is perfect for fishing because waves slowly rolled into the land, drawing red snappers, catla, white bass, rainbow trout, and black crappie along with them. Unlike the other areas of Salina, the wind doesn't reach the lagoon. Since there wasn't wind to tangle our fishing line or blow it away, we could fish sitting down. Also, we would find starfish and huge conch shells.

Upon our arrival at our fishing area, we could smell the fresh ocean breeze and hear waves slapping against the rocks. The sun was warm, reflecting silver in the pristine azure water. Seagulls were strutting, and I watched two of them tug over a piece of fish. A few fishing boats could be seen on the horizon. Salt piles collected between rocks when the sea had receded.

Too excited to sit, we positioned ourselves along the slope of a long rock. Nelson and Jailson stood about ten feet to my left, and Adilson was about five feet to my right.

"Adilson, are you ready for this?" I asked.

He looked at me as he launched his hook.

"As ready as I can be."

"Good, because today I'm not going to skin the fish . . . I'm *sooo* winning this." I launched my hook. "Nelson! Nelson! Are you ready to lose? And just to be clear, we are no longer brothers until we get home because I'm not going to help you skin the fish or light the fire."

"Clesio, we both know you aren't going to win. When it comes to fishing, I'm the master," Jailson showed off.

Then I felt something biting on my hook, so I pulled it.

"Oh yes, baby! I caught something. Jailson, you were saying . . ."

My hands began to hurt as I pulled the rope because the fish was resisting. So I let out the line, allowing the fish to swim until it got tired, and then pulled again.

"Assistant Steven, why are we paying you so much fish if you're just going to sit there? Can I have some assistance here please? This thing is big."

Laughing, he ran and grabbed the line, while I grabbed the fish. It was a red snapper about ten pounds.

While Steven was preparing my hook, Adilson caught a white bass of about five pounds.

I held the white bass up in the air. "Nelson, look at this baby that you have to prepare."

"Don't celebrate yet. I'm about to catch mine right now," Nelson said as he launched his hook. Just as he said, a minute later, he caught two fish—a red snapper half the size of mine and a black crappie of about seven pounds.

"Clesio, do you want to rephrase what you said? Who's going to lose now?" Nelson danced.

"Yeah, I want to rephrase it—you are still losing." *I hope I'm right because if lose, I'm on my own.*

Within a few minutes, Jailson caught two more large white bass.

"Clesio, this is for you," Jailson said, holding the fish up in the air.

"Jailson, you make it really hard for people to like you. I hate you."

"Nelson, you know I was only kidding about the brother thing, right? You are always my brother, and for that reason, you are going to help me skin the fish." Everyone laughed.

"Sorry, nonbrother. See, if we were brothers, I would help you. But since we are not, you are on your own."

"Oh, that's just cold. What kind of nonbrother are you?"

After finishing, Adilson and I went to the hole to prepare the fish, while Nelson, Jailson, and Steven returned to swim. About forty minutes later, they came back.

"Good timing. I was just about to go call you guys. Some fish are done," I said, pointing to the grill.

"It smells good. You guys did a good job," Nelson said.

"If I were you, I would taste it before comment," I said, laughing.

"Knowing your cooking skills, you are absolutely right," said Nelson.

"I'm seeing that we are going to remain nonbrothers for longer than I anticipated."

He hugged me. "You know I will always be your brother."

"You know, that would be more meaningful forty minutes ago, but same here."

"Okay, enough with love. I'm hungry," Jailson said.

"I agree. Let's eat," I said.

Adilson walked to plants nearby and grabbed leaves to use as plates. "We have more fish than we can eat. We should share with other people. They may be hungry."

"Good idea," Steven said.

"People, free fi—!" I yelled.

Jailson immediately jumped and placed his hand over my mouth.

"What are you doing?" he asked. He then slowly removed his hand.

"Calling people to come eat."

"Not like that. We don't have fish to feed all of Salina. We can quietly invite children first and then we can invite other people."

"Jailson, I was wrong about you. Your brain does work sometimes."

"That's what makes life unique. We learn every day."

"Not me, I learn every other day."

Besides these great activities, every year on May 18, there would a party open for everyone. People would come from everywhere to enjoy music, games, and free food. Salina would be crowded with barely any space to walk.

Thus, Salina was a favorite place among people from São Jorge, Campana, Ponta Verde, and Galinheiro (a zone between Ponta and São Jorge). Everyone would head to Salina Beach, including Eloisa and her children and Bety and her son.

However, my brother and I had very few of these amazing experiences because soon after my father departed for the United States, Eloisa and Bety wouldn't allow us to go to Salina until we completed all their tasks. We would work from eight in the morning until six in the afternoon, and then maybe they would allow us to go to Salina. After devoting all our energy working, we would be too tired to enjoy all the fun that Salina had to offer.

One year, Nelson and I worked hard during the green season so Eloisa and Bety would allow us to go to Salina Beach for the May 18 party. Not only did we fulfill all their demands, but we also behaved to impress them so they couldn't say no when we asked. About a month before the party, I asked Bety, "If Nelson and I perform all your demands, will you allow us to go to Salina?" And she had said yes. But the answer was different when May 18 arrived.

On May 18, at about noon, Eloisa and her children were at their house getting ready. Nelson, Neminha, Bety, her son, and I were at home also getting ready. The sun was bright, and the weather was hot. People could be seen traveling toward Salina.

Bety, her son, and Neminha were in the bedroom. Nelson and I were outside.

"Look at those people going to Salina. We are going to have fun. I'm so excited." Nelson's lips stretched into a smile at my enthusiasm.

"I know. A lot people are going to be there. That's going to be awesome," he said, bug-eyed. "What clothing are you going to wear?"

"The new jeans and T-shirt Father sent me, and I'm going to wear them with my black boots. I'm going to look so *hot*," I said, radiating coolness.

Nelson laughed. "Where is Neminha?"

"She is in the room with Bety."

"Is she going?"

"I think so. I hope she is going. She needs some fun in her life."

"Look who's talking. You have so much fun in your life." Nelson smiled.

"Ha-ha, shut up, at least I'm going to have fun today."

We stepped inside to get dressed. After Nelson and I finished, as we walked out, we bumped into Bety.

"Where do you guys think you're going?" Bety said, laughing evilly. *Oh no, you must be kidding me.* I pulled Nelson behind me.

"Salina." There was fear in my voice—I knew that our excitement was coming to an end.

"No, you're not!"

"Bu . . . but you said if we met all your demands, you would let us go." My voice was rising, and I instantly felt blood boiling in my body. Nelson pinched my back, cuing me to avoid the confrontation.

"Clesio! You guys can't go! You guys still need to remove the dead plants and prepare the fields for plantation before rain." Her face was a dark cloud. "Neminha, get Matio, and let's go!" Nelson grabbed my hand and pulled me toward the bedroom.

"She promised . . . Didn't she promise?" I was desperately looking for an explanation. Nelson pulled his hair as he abruptly threw himself backward on the bed. He took a deep breath, frustrated.

"Sooo unfair," I complained.

"I know it's." Nelson sat up on the bed. "Let's go remove plants so we can at least go to the after party."

My eyes widened.

"If she didn't let us go to Salina, what makes you think she will allow us to go to the after party?"

"She didn't let us go because we have to prepare the fields, so if we finish them, then she will have no excuse but to let us go."

"That sounds too good to be true, but I'm in. We have to do it anyway." We were both changing into working clothes.

After seven hours of removing dead plants, Nelson and I returned home out of breath, dirty, starved, and exhausted. Shortly after our arrival, we saw Bety, Neminha carrying Matio, and Eloisa and her children approaching in the distance. They reached the porch, laughing and bragging about what a wonderful time they had had.

"Nelson, can you smell something burning?"

"Burning? No one is even cooking. How can something be burning?" He was confused.

"Oh, it's just me. I'm burning from inside. They are pissing me off, look at them. Look how much fun they are having."

Two hours later, everyone began to get ready for the after party. Music could be heard in the house from about ten minutes' walking distance, where the after party was held.

"Clesio, what are you waiting for? Go get ready." Nelson was already getting dressed.

"Oh no, not again. I'm not getting dressed without Bety's permission. It's painful getting dressed, thinking I'm going somewhere, and then being told that I can't go. I hate it."

"Oh, one of us has to go ask her." His tone indicated that I should be the one. I turned slowly toward him, looked him in the eye, and tapped him on the shoulder.

"Let me know how it goes." I walked outside. He followed me.

"Come on, man, just ask her."

"No can do. You are the one who came up with the idea, so you ask her."

"Fine, I will." Hesitating, he hobbled into Bety's room.

I looked at my trembling hands as I hoped she would say yes.

But a minute later, Bety stormed out toward me, wearing a look of frigid anger.

"Clesio, you can't go because you have to babysit Matio."

I tightened my lips. My blood turned to ice in my veins. I tried to speak, but I couldn't articulate my thoughts. Trying to maintain calm, I collapsed on a bench near the water tank until they all left except Nelson and me.

I wasn't so mad about not going to the after party. I was furious about babysitting. Even worse, she only left enough food for Matio and no food for Nelson and me although our last meal had been at eleven that morning. Matio immediately began crying, asking for his mother. Irritated, I tried playing with him to distract his mind, but he continued to cry. An hour later, Nelson became annoyed and went to sleep in my sister's room, leaving me alone with Matio. I carried him and slowly moved around the room while gently patting his back, hoping he would fall asleep. But his crying continued nonstop.

"Shut up!" I yelled as I dropped him on the bed. He stopped crying instantly and began shaking. I looked into his fearful eyes and felt guilty. I sat next to him, slightly leaned, and hugged him. "I'm sorry. I'm so sorry. It isn't your fault." I could feel his heart accelerating. Tears began rolling down my face. A few minutes later, we both fell asleep, hugging each other.

CHAPTER 12

To the United States

Our lives changed the moment Immigration scheduled Neminha, Nelson, and me to receive our visas.

We suddenly became visible. When we walked on the streets, people invited us into their homes, feeding us and oftentimes just wanting to talk to us. People who witnessed us being abused without doing anything about it now wanted to share cookies with us. People who rejected us as friends now wanted to become our best friends. People who before hearing the news barely recognized me now would invite me to play soccer with them.

Our neighbors weren't the only ones who began treating us better. Even Bety and Eloisa started respecting us. Neminha wasn't expected to do the household chores any longer. Nelson and I weren't sent to work on the farm and in the field. No one abused us, and we were even allowed to go wherever we wished, whenever we desired. Bety and Eloisa began to involve us in their fun activities, such as playing cards. Eloisa even threw us a party to celebrate our good news.

When I was first told about my journey to the United States, I immediately cried, while my siblings celebrated. I thought about how close I had come to ending my life. I realized the five-year-old who never gave up was now seeing that perseverance paid off. I understood how one decision can impact one's life. If I had given up and committed suicide, I would have missed out this an incredible opportunity. The voice of my mother as well as the spirit of my grandmother kept me alive through difficult times. Now I learned that it didn't matter how hard people kept me down; what really mattered was how strong I kept getting up. Because that five-year-old refused to be broken, I was now a proud winner.

Three weeks after we learned about our visas, Bety was doing Neminha's hair in the living room. Eloisa, her children, our friends Jailson and Romario, cousins Steven and Adilson, and Nelson and I were sitting outside on the porch. The air was warm, and the full moon lit the yard like daylight. The next day, we would leave for the island of Praia, where we would wait two weeks for our visas to be processed and then fly to the United States. Neighbors could be seen and heard on their porches, and some were constantly arriving to say goodbye.

"How does it feel, knowing that you will soon be in the United States?" Jailson asked.

"It feels good and unreal," I replied.

Jailson nodded. He was really excited for us, but sad at the sometime.

"I can't believe you will not be here tomorrow."

"I know. I can't wait."

"São Jorge is going to be empty without you, at least for me. I'm going to miss you guys." He looked away as his head dropped.

"Oh no, I can't cry. I have already promised Nelson I won't cry." Jailson smiled and hugged me.

"Promised Nelson what?" Nelson interjected while abandoning his conversation with Eloisa and Steven.

"That I'm not going to cry," I answered.

"You are saying that now. Wait until tomorrow and you will see," Steven said.

"That's what I told him," Nelson argued.

"Clesio, tomorrow, when you realize I'm not leaving with you, you will cry hopelessly," Steven stated, smiling.

"Okay, we will see. Remember, I'm a strong guy."

"Yeah right," Nelson disagreed. He slid to sit between Jailson and me. "Clesio," he continued, "doesn't cry for big things. I mean, you can slice him with an electric cord or even break all bones, he will not cry. But when it comes to emotional things, he's the first to cry." Speechless, I instantly stormed inside, and Nelson followed me, dazed. "What is wrong?"

"Nothing."

"I know something is wrong. I know when something is bothering you."

"Well, I'm fine."

"Tonight is our last night here. We need to spend time with them."

"Actually, Nelson. Tonight is our last night here, and yet we are still talking about the stupid electric cord. Every time I hear *electric cord*, it makes me jump out of my skin. Don't you get it? I'm tormented by that damn thing." I raised my voice.

"I'm so sorry. I didn't know it bothers you so much. I will stop saying it," Nelson apologized inarticulately. "Let's go back out there and spend time with them."

I took a deep a breath. "Okay, let's go."

About two hours later, Eloisa reminded us it was growing late. "It's almost eleven. You guys should get some rest. It's going to be a long day tomorrow."

"Jailson and Steven should sleep over," I suggested.

"Did you actually believe I was going to leave?" Steven said, walking towards our bedroom. Nelson, Jailson, and I followed.

"No, not anymore, I don't."

We took two mattresses, put them on the floor side by side, and slept. At about 2:00 a.m., I tapped on my brother.

"Nelson, Nelson."

"What?"

"I can't sleep."

"Just try."

"I have been trying for three hours now, and it isn't working."

"Clesio, it's almost morning. Can you please just wait until then?"

At 5:00 a.m. I stepped outside. It was still dark and a little chilly. I grabbed an old sweater on top of the water tank, wrapped it around my shoulders, and sat on a long concrete bench near the water tank. *I can't believe I'm just a few hours away from leaving this horrible life. No more beatings, no more work, no more sleeping outside, and no more hunger. Finally, I'm going to have a good life. I can go back to school and become a successful man, and my mother will be so proud of me. My mother can finally hug and whisper in my ear that she is proud of me. Most importantly, I am going to live with my father, who will care about me.*

A few minutes later, Nelson came outside and sat beside me.

"You can't sleep, huh? Can you believe you are a few hours away from this horrible life?" he asked.

I instantly turned to him. "Get out of my head." One of his eyebrows rose.

"What are you talking about?"

"I was just thinking the same thing. Getting away from this life. I can't wait anymore. I meant it when I said I'm not going to cry. This isn't worth crying over. I'm glad to get out of here, not sad."

"We are all glad to leave this place, but it's sad to leave our friends behind."

"Point taken, but our friends' lives aren't half as devastated as ours. They live with their parents, who care about them. We also deserve to live with someone who cares about us." He reached and hugged me.

"You're right . . . What are you going to do until we leave?"

"Well, we aren't leaving until noon, so I will walk around the neighborhood and say goodbye."

****

By 11: 00 a.m., the sun was high in the sky. Loud music was playing at my grandmother's, and people were back on their porches waiting for our departure.

"He is here! He is here!" Jelson, Eloisa's son, yelled, running toward the room, where Bety was helping Neminha get ready.

Neminha, followed by Bety, came out. "Where have you been? We were looking everywhere for you!" Neminha yelled, holding her hair to one side.

"I was saying goodbye to the neighbors."

"You have less than one hour to get ready. If you don't hurry up, we will leave you behind!"

"Don't worry, I already took a shower, and Bety ironed my clothing this morning, so I can get ready in half an hour."

"Good." My sister and Bety went back to the room.

Forty minutes later, Nelson, Neminha, and I were ready to leave. I hauled our luggage outside.

"Let me help," Steven offered. "I guess this is it." *Come on, Clesio, no crying.* "I'm going to miss you guys so much. You always make me feel special. I don't know what I'm going to do without you guys."

"Come on, man, that's not fair," I said as tears filled my eyes. "I'm not supposed to cry."

Steven gave me a big hug before Jailson pulled him away and hugged me.

"Please stay in touch. Don't forget about our friendships," Jailson said, crying.

"Come on, Clesio, we have to go. We are late," Nelson urged me. I hugged Bety and Eloisa.

Jailson and Steven carried our luggage to the road. People from the neighborhood met us along the way to hug us and say their last words. Halfway down the road, Nelson and Neminha stopped and took their last look. But I didn't even pause for a moment.

The red van we had rented to take us to the local airport in São Filipe was waiting in the road. People surrounded it, waving and yelling goodbye. Once we reached the road, I wiped my tears. Nelson looked at me and smiled. I entered the van and made my way to the back, while my siblings were still saying goodbye to those people surrounding the van. I slid the window open, and people started extending their arms in to touch me for the last time. A moment later, my siblings finally entered the van. Neminha took the front seat, while Nelson sat next to me.

"I thought you said you wouldn't cry," he mocked, laughing.

"Nelson, can it wait until we get to Praia?"

"No, but I will try."

"Talking about Praia, Clesio, are you excited?" Neminiha investigated. "You will see your mother very soon."

"Yes, I'm very excited and scared."

"Scared? Scared of what?"

"Neminha, I don't know what to expect. I haven't seen her for seven years."

"That's a long time. It's like meeting her all over again," Nelson said, tapping on my back.

"Nelson, shut up. You think you are helping, but in reality, you are really not," I uttered.

"There is nothing to be afraid of. This is supposed to be a happy moment," Nelson tried to comfort me.

"There are a lot to be afraid of. First of all, I can barely remember my mother's face. So, I won't be able to recognize her at the airport. Do you know how embarrassing that is? A son can't even recognize a loving mother. I feel ashamed just saying it."

"Clesio, you are overthinking this. I'm sure you will fine." Neminha felt symphathy.

"I think my only solution is to exit the airplane very slowly and wait until someone runs toward me. The first person who runs toward me will be my mother."

"I just hope the first person isn't a male because it's pretty weird to have a guy as a mother," Nelson said, laughing.

I looked at him and shook my head. "I don't know what to say to you, man. Neminha, any comment on that?"

Neminha turned her head to face us and lowered her sunglasses below her nose. "Nope." She then fixed her sunglasses and turned around.

Approximately an hour and a half later, the van pulled up at the airport. We hauled our luggage to the check-in area and grabbed snacks before our flight. I was hungry, but food wouldn't pass down my throat. I couldn't sit still. Too many things were happening too fast at the same time—I was excited for my first plane ride; for being less than an hour away from seeing my mother; and for being only a couple of weeks away from traveling to the United States. Astonished, I paced back and forth in the terminal.

"Clesio, sit down. We are about to leave. You keep walking up and down like a crazy person," Neminha demanded.

"I'm too excited to sit. I have something inside of me, kicking and yelling 'Let's go, let's go!'" I explained as I squeezed between Nelson and Neminha.

"All passengers going to Praia, please get ready. We will be ready for boarding in five minutes," an airline employee announced a moment later. I instantly got up. I could feel my hands and legs shaking.

"That's us, that's us, that's us," I celebrated, jumping up and down.

"Clesio, I totally understand you are excited, but if you are going to act like that, either stand twenty feet away or warn me so I can move away from you, while pretending I don't know you," Nelson said as he grabbed and guided me to sit down.

"Yeah, Clesio, that was pretty embarrassing," Neminha agreed, nodding.

"I see you guys don't appreciate my good moves." I smiled.

"Yeah, Clesio, that's exactly it," Neminha said sarcastically. We laughed.

"All passengers to Praia, please begin boarding now," the employee announced again. *That's it. Goodbye, Fogo. Hello, Praia, here I come.* Nelson, Neminha, and I boarded the plane. *Oh my God, this plane is big. How can it fly? How can it stay up in the air?*

"Clesio, Clesio, are you okay? You look distracted," Neminha asked, her eyes wide.

"Huh? Yeah, I'm okay. Nelson, can I please sit by the window?"

"Why is that?"

"Because this is my first time on a plane. So, I won the right to explore the nature. I want to see how the ground looks from the air." I reached to store my carry-on in the overhead compartment.

"Bro, the last time I checked, I have never been on a plane either. I would love to explore as well."

"But you are the big brother. You're supposed to consider my comfort first."

"You know what, I really hate you," Nelson said as he moved out of his seat to allow me to sit by the window.

"I really love you, too." I leaned and hugged him.

"Get off me, get off me. I didn't say anything about loving you."

"Okay, lovebirds, cut it out," Neminha said while she sat down.

"Okay, is it just me, or do you guys also think it's amazing that this big plane will soon be up in the air without falling down?" I looked at them for an answer.

"No, it's just you," Neminha responded.

"Wow, that was cold." Without giving her any more attention, I leaned forward, looking out the window.

About twenty minutes later, we took off. I watched the ground getting smaller and smaller, the buildings getting thinner, and thinner and cars vanishing away. *After all the years of anguishing, I'm finally flying away. What a life I had! I'm so glad I didn't give up. When I arrive in the United States, I will reenroll at school so I can show my tormenters that I will be successful no matter what.*

Approximately twenty-five minutes later, we landed at Praia Airport.

"Clesio, are you ready to see your mother?" Neminha asked.

"No."

"What are you waiting for?"

"My body to stop shaking."

"Don't worry, you will be fine."

As I attempted to grab my carry-on, Nelson took it from me. He was aware of my shaking body, my sweaty forehead, and my heavy breaths.

"You have enough to worry about," he said, signaling me to go first.

Standing at the exit, I swallowed, trying to moisturize my dried mouth while repeatedly rubbing my hands against each. Right before stepping outside, I took a deep breath, trying to clam myself down. Once out, I looked to my right, left, and then straight, but I didn't see anyone running toward me.

"I don't see your mother," Nelson said softy.

"I don't see her either. Maybe she didn't come." As soon as I closed my mouth, I saw a woman running toward us. "Neminha, is that her? Should I run toward her?"

"Yes!"

"Is the yes it's her or yes to run?" I asked nervously.

"Both. Just run already!"

I ran toward her with open arms and hugged her. I instantly had goose bumps because the hug was so unreal—it felt like magic. I could feel joy building in my heart.

"I missed you so much," my mother expressed, squeezing me. I could hear the crying in her voice.

"I missed you, too."

She slowly released me and extended her hand to greet my siblings.

"Are you guys excited to go to America?" my mother quizzed, as she wrapped her arm around my shoulders.

"Yes, we are very excited. I can barely wait," Nelson answered.

"When are you guys leaving?"

"In two weeks. We still need to pick up our visas at Immigration," Neminha responded.

"Where are you guys staying?"

"We are staying at our aunt's house."

"Which one?"

"Aunt Laura. She is my father's sister."

"Oh, Laura, I see her around sometimes."

"Clesio, you should go with your mother, and I will pick you up tomorrow," Neminha proposed.

"Okay, I will go with her," I replied.

My mother smiled and tousled my hair. I turned to Nelson and Neminha and hugged them goodbye.

"We are going to get you tomorrow, okay?" Nelson said. I could see sadness through his eyes.

"Okay."

My mother and I left in a taxi for her house while my siblings went to Laura's.

"How have you been?" My mother gently pulled me and laid my head on her chest. *Clesio, if you tell her the truth, she will get worried.*

"I have been good."

"How were Bety and Eloisa treating you?" she investigated as if she already knew the answer. Just thinking about my past, always made my heart twinge.

"Good." She examined my body, lifting my shirt to see my chest and back.

"How come your body is covered with scars?" *I can't tell her that Bety beat me with an electric cord. She will go crazy.*

"I fell," I said quickly, trying to pull my shirt back down.

"Fell? These look like marks from beating. I know Eloisa and Bety aren't saints," she uttered as she pulled my shirt up again to take a closer look.

"Can we please not talk about this? I am trying to leave my past behind and create a new life."

"Okay." I could sense sorrow in her voice. She finally let my shirt go and settled back for the ride.

Later that day, my mother took me to eat at a popular restaurant a few minutes drive from her domicile. She also gave me tours of the most popular places in Praia. We walked on the Kebra Kanela Beach for about twenty minutes, and lastly she took me shopping.

At bedtime, she brewed me a cup of tea to help me digest my food. She then prepared my bed and waited until I got in to cover me.

"Have a great night's sleep and lots of sweet dreams," she said as she kissed my forehead.

"You too," I replied, electrified.

Early the next day, I walked into the kitchen to find my mother already placed my breakfast on the table. *This is what I have been missing all my life. Not only was I not dragged out of bed in the morning, but I also get to have a real breakfast.* My mother waited until I brushed my teeth to have breakfast with me.

"How was your night's sleep?" she asked, smiling.

"Great." Wearing a joyful smile, she buttered my bread and cut it into three pieces, making them easy to eat, and poured mango juice in my glass.

Although I was excited to travel to America, I didn't want these moments to end. But time seemed to fly by and before I knew it was time to depart for the United States of America.

On October 24, 2004, Neminha, Nelson, Laura, my mother, and I arrived at the Praia Airport at 5:03 a.m.

"I think the feeling is starting to kick in. It feels real now," I murmured after check-in.

I quickly confirmed the information on my boarding pass as we sat in a lounge a few steps away from the waiting room.

"Look at me, I'm shaking," Nelson pointed out. "Have you seen the plane? It's huge."

"I know. It's the air *Titanic*."

"What is air *Titanic*?" Laura asked confused.

"Don't ask. Clesio is being stupid. He's referring to the movie *Titanic*," Neminha explained.

"Neminha, I don't know what you are talking about. I thought that was clever," Nelson argued.

"I still don't get it," said Laura.

"The plane is the air Titanic because it's huge like Titanic, and it travels in the air. There you have it, air Titanic," Nelson patiently explained.

"Oh, I see," Laura replied.

"So sad," Neminha said, shaking her head.

"I still think it was funny," Nelson urged.

"Thank you, Nelson. At least, someone around here appreciates a good sense of humor." I said, looking directly at Neminha.

"Attention, passengers to the United States, please form a line, and we'll begin security check-in momentarily," an airline employee announced.

"Oh my God, it's happening." I mused as we stood up.

My mother inched toward me and hugged me. I was crying inconsolably. As I hugged my mother, I became doubtful about my new journey.

"Clesio, we have to board now," Neminha said, pulling my hand. My heart felt like it was being ripped apart.

"Go, Clesio," my mother ordered, crying. I squeezed her.

"I don't want to go anymore," I declared still crying.

"You have to. Don't worry, one day we will be together again. But you have to go now." She released me.

"I'm going to miss you so much,"

"I will miss you too." She waved as Neminha pulled me toward the gate.

CHAPTER 13

Life in America

Neminha, Nelson, and I arrived at Logan Airport in Boston at about 11:00 p.m. since we had a nondirect flight from Sal, one of the ten Cape Verde Islands, to live with my father, his wife Linda, and her three children—Joelma, Jamira, and Paul. My father owned a three-family house in Boston, Massachusetts. The third floor was rented by a Spanish family, while the second floor was rented by my father's aunt Melia, her husband Antero, and their children—Tay, Altobele, Geovanny, Placido, and Camila. We occupied the first floor and the basement—guys in the basement and girls on the first floor.

My father and Linda met us at the airport. When I first saw my father, I ran toward him and gave him a big hug. In that hug, I felt something I had never felt before under the "care" of my father's relatives—loved and secure.

"Welcome to the United States!" my father greeted us. "How was the flight?"

"Long," I answered.

"Yes! I ran out of movies to watch," Nelson added. We laughed. As we walked through Logan Airport to the parking lot, I admired how huge Logan was compared to the airport back in Cape Verde; suddenly, the giant planes in Cape Verde seemed tiny. I had never seen anything like it before. Amazed, I looked around, appreciating all the technology—escalators, vending machines, automatic doors, and parking machines that gave us the exact change.

"Papa, how in the world do these machines know how to give us the exact change?" I asked, confused. My mouth still dropped, I looked at Nelson in disbelief.

"They install magnetic ink on the bills and scanners on the machine to determine the exact money one has inserted into each machine," Linda explained.

"Wow, clever!" *I love this country already* . . . "Nelson, how do you feel about that?"

"Feel about what?" he asked, bug-eyed.

"A machine, smarter than you. That must be so painful to learn, isn't it?" Glaring into his eyes and slowly patting my lips with my forefinger, I waited for an answer, trying my best not to laugh.

"Like you are smarter than the machine."

"Well, at least, I know how to give change."

"That was one time. Can you please let it go?" Nelson said with exhaustion.

"What is he talking about?" Linda interjected.

"One day, I sold him candy and accidently gave him fifty cents extra change," he explained impatiently.

"Clesio, did you refund his money?" Linda asked.

"Yeah right! You are funny. That was my lunch money."

"Put on your jacket on. It's cold," my father suggested, handing us jackets.

"Oh no, I don't need a jacket." I denied the offer.

"It's cold outside," Linda warned me.

"It cannot be that cold. Plus my skin is cold-proof."

"Okay, we'll see." She looked at my father and smiled.

My father placed our luggage on two separate carts and pushed one, while Nelson pushed the other to the car.

As I walked out, a cold air blew in my face. "Oh, it's cold!" I screamed. "I changed my mind. I think I want my jacket now. I feel like I'm on the *Titanic*." I sprinted toward my father, snatched the jacket from his shoulder and quickly wore it. Walking outside was mind-blowing—tall buildings, jillion of cars, paved highways, and lighting everywhere.

"How is Cape Verde?" my father asked as we got into the car.

"Cape Verde? What is Cape Verde?" I asked. Everyone turned and stared at me.

"Clesio, wait until you exit from the airport parking lot before you forget your own country because Immigration can still send you back," Nelson said. We laughed.

"You guys are funny," Linda said, laughing and tapping her hand on the dashboard.

"They always act like this even in difficult times," Neminha answered. "I remember the day Eloisa sent us in the dark to bring vines to a storage shed near the house. You know how frustrating they are to carry. I cried like a little girl, while Nelson and Clesio were making fun of each other."

"On the way here I promised myself that I'm going to forget everything that happened in Cape Verde and begin a new life," I disclosed. I looked out the window for the rest of the ride home, enjoying the beauty of the city.

We arrived home around midnight. Instantly after I entered the house, I could smell fresh air. Admiring the shining hardwood floors and the golden walls, the matching curtains, and the large ornamental vase in the corner of the living room, I curiously surveyed around. In the living room was a small table with a vase of fresh flowers to celebrate our arrival. Three white couches surrounded the table. A photo of my father, taken when he was twenty years old in the army, hung on the wall.

"Who is that?" Nelson asked, looking directly at the picture.

"Me," my father answered, proudly. My sister's mouth dropped, and she inched toward the picture for a closer look. My father followed her.

"No, that's not you!" she exclaimed. Nelson and my father sat down on the couch. My sister continued to stare at the photo. Looking at the lights outside, I imagined how the streets would look in the daylight.

"Papa, are you going to give us an outside tour tomorrow morning?" I asked, impressed with the little I could see. He turned and looked at Linda, but she was looking down, so she didn't see him. He then looked directly into my eyes.

"I work in the morning, but maybe after work," he replied in a soft voice.

Awkward silence riddled the room as we ran out of things to say. To break the awkward moment, Linda, smiling, stood up and asked, "Are you guys hungry?"

"Yeah, I'm. Starving actually. I was so excited on the trip that I couldn't eat," Nelson answered. Everyone headed to the kitchen. The movement of the traffic and the warmly lit houses mesmerized me.

"Clesio?" Nelson yelled. His voice sounded disappointed. "Come eat. Outside isn't going anywhere."

"Are you sure?" I asked as I caught up to them. "If I don't find it there tomorrow, we are going to have a big problem, young man." Everyone laughed.

I sat between Nelson and my father, and Neminha sat at the head of the table. Linda served us steak, white rice, beans, and salad. After serving, she squeezed between Neminha and Nelson.

"How do you like the meal?" Linda asked, looking at me.

"It's delicious food. I can taste America in my mouth," I joked, smiling.

"I can't even remember the last time I had food this tasty," Nelson said.

"I can remember the last time," I responded.

"When?"

"Never." Everyone laughed.

"Do you guys want any dessert?" Linda offered, excited.

Neminha's eyebrows rose. She looked at me, and I looked at Nelson for any hint, but his puzzled face offered no help.

"Dessert? What is dessert?" I asked, confused.

"Something sweet, normally ice cream with fudge."

"Wow. Am I dreaming? Someone please pinch me." Nelson reached and pinched. "Ouch!" I screamed.

"No, you're awake," Nelson said.

"Figure of speech, dude. I wasn't being literal. Anyways, Linda, you should've told me there would be dessert! I would've saved room for it. I'm too full now." I rubbed my belly. Linda and my father smiled.

A moment later, Neminha, conditioned as the housekeeper, removing plates from the table to wash them in the sink. I was distracted, looking around. Stove, dishwasher, microwave, and toaster—all items that I had never seen in my life. I felt so happy to be full for the first time.

Linda was the first to speak. "I'm going to bed because I have to go to work early in the morning. David, why don't you give them a tour of the rest of the house?"

Nelson couldn't wait until seeing the rest of the house. "Yeah, I want to see the basement." He noticed I was distracted, so he kicked me to get my attention. My father led us to the basement, and we descended the stairs.

There were two bedrooms—one near the staircase and the other all the way at the end of the hall. There was also a large TV area, a run-down bathroom, and a room containing a huge furnace. A loud noise could be heard from the furnace room.

"What's that noise?" I quizzed curiously.

"It's the heating machine. It keeps us warm," my father explained.

"Is it going to interfere with our sleep?"

"You can barely hear it when you close your bedroom door. Plus, the noise isn't constant." He sounded worried that we might be disappointed. He walked to the bedroom near the staircase. "This is the room for you guys." Nelson and I looked at each other, trying to hide our disappointment. As our father stepped into the room, Nelson placed his finger across his mouth, indicating for me not to say anything. My sister's eyebrows went up, clearly worried she might have to room with one of Linda's daughters.

"Where is my bedroom?" she asked inaudible.

"You have your own upstairs." Her face broke into a smile. Nelson and I concealed the grimace on our faces.

Next my father walked to the TV area and pointed toward the room at the end.

"That's Paul's room. He's sleeping now. You guys will meet him tomorrow. That's about it. You guys make yourself at home. I have to rest because I also work early in the morning." Shortly after, my father and sister went upstairs. As soon as they left, I broke loose.

"I thought we would have our own rooms," I told my brother. Without saying a word, he went to our room, and I followed. "This isn't fair. Paul has his own room. Why can't we have our own rooms? Huh?"

He walked up to me and gently placed his hand on my shoulder. "Can't you please stop complaining? Isn't that what you asked for?"

"What do you mean what I asked for? What did I ask for?"

"Remember that day Eloisa forced us to carry sand?"

"Yes, what about it?"

"Remember, you said you only wanted to have a normal life with someone who cares about you. Here is your wish. Appreciate what you have now."

He removed his hand and went to take shower in the bathroom downstairs while I showered upstairs. During the shower, I realized how ungrateful I sounded.

"You're right. I guess I'm just scared." I said when we returned to the room.

"Scared? Scared of what?"

I walked to our bed and sat on the edge opposite from him. "You know, every time I move to new places, things always seem to take wrong turns. I'm afraid this astonishing life will not last."

"This is our father we're talking about, not the heartless creatures we grew up with. He cares about us. He will protect us."

"I just hope you are right!"

"You are worried over nothing."

"Maybe you are right."

"Let's get some sleep so we can wake up early in the morning to check outside," he proposed as he turned off the light.

I lay there and thought about the heartrending movements of life and the horror of the last beating with the electric cord. But no matter what would have happened, I vowed to myself to fight until the end to honor the five-years-old who survived all the catastrophic journeys of my life. Could life in the United States be another battle?

From the way those expatriates who returned to visit family in Cape Verde described the United States, I thought I would have my own room, and I would never have to work again, or even if I did, it wouldn't be as hard, and I would get paid for it. Some visitors told me that in the United States, I would find money on the floor, free furniture everywhere I turn, and people would get rich easily. Based on these descriptions, I imagined the United States as a paradise, a place where I would never suffer again and a place where, finally, I would be happy. When the idea of immigrating to the United States was first introduced to us, I could barely wait to escape abuse, hardship, and the hostility of my antagonists. So was I wrong? Am I at risk of reliving these catastrophes?

Even though I didn't find money on the ground, and the only furniture found outside was cast-off furniture, life in the United States was much better than in Cape Verde. Just going to bed without worrying about getting up early in the morning to work was an incredible feeling. It felt unreal spending day in and day out without people ordering me around or abusing me. In addition, in contrast to Cape Verde, where I would have only one or two meals a day, in the United States, I could eat anytime as much as I desired.

Finally, I was having fun. On weekends, I would spend time on the second floor, playing PlayStation with my cousins Placido, Geovanny, Tay, and Altobele. Occasionally, they took Neminha, Nelson, and me to the movie theaters and bowling alleys. We also played soccer outdoor together. My life began to have some light and direction. I felt wanted and loved. Family and friends would invite me out and sometimes to even spend the night at their homes. My cousin Gil, my father's nephew, would often take me to places, such as museums. My father and Linda would also sometimes bring us to shopping centers to buy us clothing and personal needs.

Most importantly, I began pursuing my dream. Within two months, my father enrolled me in Jeremiah E. Burke High School. I was placed in the ninth grade, but because of my determination and hard work, I was able to complete ninth and tenth grades in the same year. I used to ask Joelma, Linda's daughter, to teach me how to read every day, and when Joelma was not able to, I would go to the second floor to ask my cousin Placido to teach me English. To improve my English even further, I signed up for Saint Peter's afterschool program. I would go to school in the morning and the afterschool in the evening. At Saint Peter's, I made friends with whom I would play soccer after we finished our homework. My triumph was quickly recognized when t began earning As and Bs in school.

For seven months, I considered myself lucky for having an opportunity to alter my life for better. Now, I had purpose to waking up each morning, not because I was forced, but simply because I was working to empower my future.

But just as I projected, in June, only eight months after our arrival, I began noticing some changes. One night, at about eleven o'clock, Nelson, Geovanny, and I were watching the sequel to *Home Alone* in the basement, when we heard footsteps rapidly descending the basement's staircase. I leaned forward and forced my eyes to see the shadow stride toward us. Nelson paused the movie before my father turned on the light.

"You guys need to stop going upstairs after 10:00 p.m.!" he shouted, still carrying his lunch container.

Surprised and confused, Nelson and I looked at each other.

"Why? What did we do wrong?" I asked, shocked.

"You are making too much noise upstairs. You know, Linda has to get up at five in the morning to go to work!" he yelled as he stood in front of the television. Geovanny left speechless.

"But we barely go upstairs, and when we do, we're always quiet. We understand that Linda wakes up early," Nelson responded, hesitating.

"I'm going to keep my eyes on you two!" our father left.

"What was that all about?" I asked Nelson, shaking after my father successfully made his way up the stairs. Nelson shook his head, indicating that he didn't know. As I got up to leave, Nelson grabbed my hand.

"Where are you going?"

"I'm going to bed."

"What about the movie?"

"I don't feel like watching a movie anymore, Nelson." I went to bed while Nelson remained watching the movie.

Things were gradually getting worse. Two weeks later, a similar event occurred. My father interrupted my sleep in the middle of the night, knowing that I had to go to school early the next morning. He entered our bedroom and immediately turned on the light, causing me to wake up. He walked to my side of the bed and removed my blanket. Half asleep, I sat on the bed.

"What's going on?" I mumbled, recalling my life with Mary.

"Ever since you two came here, I have been receiving complaints about you two!"

My eyes widened, trying to follow what he was saying.

"From whom? Complaining about what? We go to school early in the morning, and I go to Saint Peter's right after school. By the time I get home to take a shower and eat, it's my bedtime. So I don't understand what we're doing wrong," I kindly explained.

"The sink is full of dirty dishes. Why don't you guys wash your dishes after you eat?"

"I wash my dishes, and sometimes, I even wash all dishes before I go to bed. Neminha also does the dishes before she goes to bed. So I don't understand how can there possibly be dirty dishes."

"Well, I don't know?"

"What am I supposed to do?" I looked into his eyes, waiting for an answer.

"When you find dirty dishes in the sink, wash them even if they aren't yours. That way, we can eliminate some problems."

"We do that every night. Neminha, Nelson, and I wash all the dirty dishes before we go to bed."

"If you guys are washing them, how come I find dirty dishes in the sink every night? That doesn't make sense."

"I don't know. We wash the dishes before we go to bed. If you want, I will set an alarm every thirty minutes to police the sink and find out how it's producing dirty dishes," I said, irritated, as I lay back down. Without saying another word, he left.

"What was that all about?" Nelson asked.

"I knew you weren't sleeping. You saw me struggling here, but you didn't back me up."

"I didn't back you up because I didn't want it to turn into a major argument."

"I have a bad feeling about this. This life is starting to feel like life with Eloisa. These situations seem they are only getting worse," I stated, hoping that I was wrong.

"Don't say that. Papa will never abuse us." He tapped on my back. "Let's get some sleep. Don't worry. Everything will be fine."

"I hope you are right."

Nelson turned off the light, and I lay there wondering, is *this going to stop, or is this the beginning of another chapter of a horrible life?*

Slowly the answers to these questions became clear. I realized that neither my father nor the United States was what I had imagined. One night when I had returned from my Saint Peter's class at 9:30 p.m., my father informed me that we would have a family meeting in half an hour in his room. At ten Neminha, Nelson, and I assembled in front of his door.

"Come in. You guys can sit on the bed," my father offered calmly.

My father and Linda were lying on the bed. In my father's room was a huge bed, occupying the majority of the room. On the left was a brown dresser, and on the right was a nightstand. A computer sat on a desk between the dresser and the television. My sister sat on one side of the bed near my father. Nelson and I leaned against the wall. *Home Alone* was playing, unwatched, on the television at the foot of the bed. While leaning on the wall, I wondered if I had done anything wrong to provoke this meeting. I could hear Nelson's heavy breathing. My father reached for the television remote and muted the sound.

"I called all of you here for this meeting because it's time for you guys to find jobs. I'm not going to provide for your personal needs anymore. You guys need to learn how to advocate for yourself: clothing, lotion, shampoo and conditioner, toothpaste and toothbrush, and the list goes on. But you get the idea." He paused and looked at each one of us. "Also," he continued, "all of you are responsible to repay the money I spent on your plane tickets." My father made the request abruptly.

Linda nodded her agreement while he was speaking. Nelson's eyes widened. He was provoked to say something but thought it would only made the matter worse, so he remained silent.

"What about my school? Work will interfere with school." I worried.

"Clesio, you can go to school and work at the same time," he raised his voice.

Nelson cleared his throat. "How are we going to even get to school and work if we don't know our way around?"

My father sat up. As he was getting up, my heart palpitated. He looked at all of us, but I lowered my gaze to avoid eye contact.

"You will learn!" my father demanded.

As I opened my mouth to confront him, my brother kicked me, to hold back. Angry and furious, I left the room.

The next day, Neminha and Nelson went on a job search. Soon after, Nelson managed to find a job at McDonald's, while Linda helped my sister land one at the sausage factory where she worked. A few days later, my father discovered that I wasn't searching for an employment. He, instead, went to the McDonald's where Nelson worked to find me a job himself. Coincidently, the manager was a friend of his.

One day, he interrupted my sleep at midnight, when he came home from work, to break the news.

"Clesio, I spoke with the manager at McDonald's, and he said to bring your documentation tomorrow. Go ready to work because you may start tomorrow." He smiled.

I can't afford to leave school now.

I sat up on the bed, still half asleep. "I can't work because I have to go Saint Peter's to improve my English and grades."

"People who don't work cannot live in my house, Clesio. If you don't want to work, grab your stuff and leave." He slammed the door as he stormed out.

To avoid problems, I reported to work the next day immediately after school.

Employment had a significant impact on my grades because there was little or no time for homework. My school day lasted from 8:30 a.m. until 2:20 p.m. Bus route 16 had a stop near our house and another very near the school. However, I couldn't rely on it because it ran late most of the time. I often would end up walking. There was no bus at all to connect my house to work. As a result, I had to run home, a distance of 1.6 miles, right after school to eat and change, then run another 1.7 miles to work. By the time I walked home from work, it would be close to one in the morning. Most of the time, I wouldn't be able to go to bed until 3:00 a.m. to 4:00 a.m. but still had to wake up at 6:00 a.m. every day to make it to school on time.

Working wasn't the only thing in my father's mind. In the late summer, my father introduced a new rule, a curfew for Nelson and me, preventing us from going anywhere except work. One day, immediately after I returned from Saint Peter's at 9:30 p.m., as I attempted to turn the key in the door, my father opened the door in and snapped at me.

"Where have you been? Do you have any idea what time it is?" my father asked, furious. My eyebrows raised as my eyes widened.

"I went to Saint Peter's to get help with my homework," I answered, grabbing the knob of the kitchen door, leading to the basement.

"Saint Peter's until this time?" he raised his voice, doubting me.

I turned around and took a few steps toward him.

"Yes, I'm performing poorly in school because I don't have time to study anymore, so I'm going to Saint Peter's on my days off, trying to improve my grades."

"Do you think I'm stupid? Since when does Saint Peter's run until this time?" he challenged me as though he knew Saint Peter's hours of operation.

"You don't believe me, do you? Where else could I be? Selling drugs on the streets?"

He shrugged before saying "I don't know. We all need to have a family meeting right now. Call Nelson and Neminha." He went to his room.

"Nelson? Nelson?" I called from the staircase.

"What?"

"Where are you?"

"Down here, in the basement."

"Is Neminha there with you?"

"Yes, what do you want?" Neminha asked.

"Can you guys come up? Family meeting."

"Oh nooo. Not a family meeting," Nelson complained. I waited for them.

"What is wrong?" Neminha stared into my eyes as if I had done something wrong.

"I don't know, but be ready because he isn't happy."

Shaking, we stumbled to his room. Linda was lying down on the bed, next to my father, who was facing the door. Neminha entered the room and sat on the bed next to my father, while Nelson and I stood in the doorway.

"You guys can come in, you know. There is room to fit all of us," my father invited us, pointing to the bed.

"No, it's okay. I will stand. I need to grow anyway," I joked.

He glared at me briefly, and rubbed his knuckles slightly as he took in a breath to start. "I called you here because I have been receiving complaints from people living upstairs that you guys are making too much noise. So from now on, you guys have to be in bed by 9:00 p.m. every day, except the days you work, of course."

"But we live in the basement. How can they possible hear the noise?" I invoked.

"I don't know, and I don't care how. Plus this way, I will have a peace of mind, knowing that you guys are safe in bed. Clesio just got home. You could easily have been killed out there," my father argued.

I clenched my teeth in frustration. "Since when do you care about our safety? You refuse to pick us up at work, so we have to walk home at 1:00 a.m. That's not safe. I'm most likely to be killed at 1:00 a.m. than 9:30 p.m."

"Clesio, I'm not here to argue with you. In this house, there are rules, and if you don't like them, just pack your bag and leave. It's that simple."

Nelson poked my back, nudging me to stop challenging my father. Neminha and Linda remained silent.

"As you said it's your house, so I am going to follow the rules." I looked directly into my father eyes. "But they don't make sense." And then I walked away.

CHAPTER 14

Love of a Monster

Yelling, trivial curfews, and employment weren't the only disappointing and unpleasant introductions into our lives. By our second February in America, life in the United States began to feel identical to the one in Cape Verde. First, I noticed that the rules applied only to Neminha, Nelson, and me. Similar to Eloisa's children, Linda's children could go anywhere at any time without any repercussion, while my siblings and I were forced to be in bed by 9:00 p.m., whether or not we were sleepy. Linda's children were even allowed to spend the night out, but the same wasn't true for us.

Also, my siblings and I were assigned house chores, whereas Linda's children weren't responsible for anything, just as it had been with Eloisa's children. My assigned chores were cleaning the basement, the staircases, and our street!

I would sweep, mop, and rearrange the entire basement. I also was responsible for cleaning the bathroom. After finishing the basement, I would sweep both the back and front staircases from the third floor down to the first. Then struggling with a large bucket of sloshing water, I would mop the front and back staircases from the third to the first floors. Once the inside cleaning was finished, I had to sweep our dead-end street from the beginning to the end.

In addition to cleaning chores, I was responsible for cementing the backyard. Attached to my father's house was a yard about twenty feet wide and sixty feet long. My father utilized the yard to plant corn and beans before we came to the United States. However, after our arrival, he decided to turn it into a cookout area.

On weekends, my father would wake me up as early as 6:00 a.m. In February, the temperature could be in the teens or single digits. Every time my father pulled off my blanket, my heart would feel as though someone was squeezing it. Irritated, I would put on three layers of clothing, grab a garden hoe and a shovel, and head to the backyard. First, I had to dig to level the ground. Then I would drive with my father in his truck and shovel in the sand and pebbles, bought from the gravel company. Back at home, I would shovel out the truck while my father would just stand there giving orders. I did this for a month until it was warm enough to pour the cement in March. If Nelson was available, he would help. During the making of the pavement, I had to mix the concrete, collected loose rocks around the yard, and poured the mixed concrete until I successfully paved the whole yard.

Spontaneously after the patio was completed, Nelson and I were drafted to repair the bathroom upstairs. I did most of the work. I had to tear apart the entire interior of the bathroom and replace everything, from floor to ceiling. That included the floor, walls, ceiling, tub, toilet, and sink. Breaking through a floor with a smash hammer is hard work. On my first day of smashing, the weight of the hammer and its impact against the floor blistered my palms. Still, even with my raw hands, I had to pick up where I had left off the next day. I hated working in the bathroom because I didn't have proper work clothes. I didn't own gloves, heavy boots, a mask, or safety goggles. Every time I hit the smash hammer against the floor, sharp pieces of tile, rock, and wood would fly into my face and eyes.

One day I came home from school, Neminha informed me that our father wanted me to resume the work on the bathroom. Furious, I changed into my jeans and sweater from the previous day. *I came to the United States to have a better life, and I end up with this. I don't have time to rest. I don't have time to eat. I don't even have time to do my damn homework.*

Without eating, I grabbed my sledgehammer, ambled into the bathroom, and locked the door. Exasperated, I surveyed around at all the breaking I had to do. I lifted and smashed the hammer against the bathtub.

"Is everything okay in there?" Neminha asked, worried.

"Yeah, everything is fine!" I lied.

As I hit the tiles, I could feel the vibration in my body, especially in my heart. One time, I used a piece of wood as leverage to lift a tile that seemed loose. As I grabbed the tile, the wood broke, causing the tile to snap off one whole fingernail. Everything went black for a few seconds.

"Puuuta!" I screamed

"Clesio?" Neminha called.

"Whaaat?" I yelled, annoyed.

"Are you okay?"

"Yes! I'm fine. Just leave me alone!"

I glanced at my bloody hand. Watching my finger bleeding was more painful than the actual pain. I sat there for a moment, wincing, trying not to cry. Both of my hands were shaking uncontrollably. I ran to the run-down bathroom in the basement to wash my bloody finger. I turned on the water and slowly brought my injured hand under the water tap. Hesitating, I attempted detaching the remaining, but the pain was too intense. With every attempt, it felt as if my finger was boiling in extremely hot water. Howling in pain, I removed the nail, tied it with a piece of old clothing, and returned to breaking.

It took me approximately a month and a half to complete the renovation. As soon as I finished the bathroom, my father and Linda locked it to prevent all the young men from using it. We were forced to use the dissatisfactory bathroom in the basement.

Once the renovation was finished, my father found a new project for me. Because water was leaking through the basement door when it rained, he decided to extend the entrance with a covered stairwell. It was necessary to dig about twenty feet to add reinforcement to the addition so it wouldn't collapse. I was ordered to work on the project during my free time, digging every weekend and on my days off from work.

My father would get angry if I failed to comply. One day, when I arrived home from school, I found a note from my father on the refrigerator, asking me to finish digging that day. I snatched the note, rubbed it in my hands, forming a ball shape, and forcibly threw it in the trash but missed. I grabbed it and tried it gain, but missed once more. Irritated, I abruptly snatched it again, opened the back door, and threw it as far as I could.

"Get out of my face." I screamed before descending to the basement to change into my old clothing.

I grabbed my tools and staggered to the workstation. After digging for three hours, the shovel handle hit my knee. Frustrated, I raised the shovel as high as I could and smashed it against the ground, and it bounced back and hit me in the face. "Goddamn!" I yelled, kicking a bucket of water, causing it to splash all over me. Hot tears immediately rolled down my face. I could feel anger building inside of me.

"Are you okay down there?" Tay asked from their back porch right above me. I turned and craned my head to look at him.

"No! I'm not okay. This is bullshit. Everything is going wrong."

"Why? What is wrong?"

"I will tell what is wrong," I raised my voice as if it was his fault. "I have no time to rest or do my homework. I have to go to school, I have to go to work, and on the weekend, I have to clean the basement, staircases, and the stupid street. And now on days off, I have to do this stupid job, while paying him fifty dollars per week. Look at my finger. It still hurts. I'm exhausted. That's what wrong."

"Yeah, I feel what you are going through, man. Your father shouldn't have you do all these work by yourself. He brought you here to have a better life, but now you're stuck doing this. You know, he could pay someone to do this kind work for cheap," Tay sympathized.

"You have no idea how awful my life has been."

"Yeah, you've only been here for a year and a half. It's a year and a half, right?"

"It will be on the twenty-fourth of this month."

"See, you've been here for less than two years, and he's making you do all this work."

"What hurts me most is that Paul never has to do anything, and Nelson only helps when he feels like it. So, I'm always the one who ends up doing all the work."

"That's not fair."

"I've never experienced fairness in my life. Honestly, I don't know how much more I can take."

"Yeah, I overheard that you guys had such a tough time with Eloisa and Bety in Cape Verde. I don't know all the details. But Nelson was talking about some of the terrible things that happened. Definitely, you shouldn't be doing this. You should be resting and focusing on school." His head dropped. I could tell he was distressed.

"Man, I thought I would finally have a better life, coming here, but it feels like I'm in Cape Verde all over again. I've been working for nearly eight months nonstop. See this yard." I pointed at the yard, about five feet away. "I finished paving it, fixed the entire bathroom, which we aren't even allowed to use, and now this. I'm wondering what is next."

"Take a break and come back to it tomorrow."

"No, I can't. My father left a note, requesting to finish it today."

"Tomorrow is Saturday. You can finish it tomorrow."

I smiled. "Yeah, you're right. I'm almost done anyways. I'll wake up early tomorrow and finish it."

"Good! Placido is playing FIFA on the PlayStation. Come upstairs, and we will play against each other."

"Sounds good. Let me take a quick shower, and I'll be right there."

We played for nearly two hours, and I lost every game. Then I headed to bed, planning to wake up early the next morning to dig.

From a heavy sleep, I felt something shaking me. I jumped and saw a shadow standing directly in front of me. He turned the light on. With my eyes half opened, I tried to understand what was happening.

"Why didn't you finish the digging?" my father yelled.

"I was tired, so I took a little break. But I will finish it early in the morning," I mumbled.

"Take a break? Or do you mean play PlayStation upstairs?" he shouted as he removed my covers. I could feel my blood turning into ice. *Seriously? You must be kidding me.*

"I didn't stop digging to play PlayStation. I stopped because I was tired, and then I went to play!" I raised my voice.

"Clesio, when I ask you to do something, I expect you to finish it. How many time do I have to repeat myself? I make the rules in this house, and you have to follow them. If you don't want to follow them, just pack your bag. You better finish the digging tomorrow. No excuses." He walked to the door, but before he exited, he halted and turned his heard toward me. "From now on, I don't want you upstairs. You are banned from going up." *Why don't you do me a favor and send me to jail? I bet I will have a better life there.*

My father was certainly getting a lot of bang for his buck. I was paying fifty dollars a week while providing a steady source of labor. At the time, the minimum wage was seven dollars per hour, so I was earning only one hundred and sixty dollars per week. With the remaining one hundred and ten dollars, I had to pay for all my other expenses, such as clothing, shoes, personal hygiene products, while helping my mother in Cape Verde. Whatever remaining amount, he could confiscate to repay for plane tickets.

In order to meet all my expenses, I extended my hours at McDonald's from eleven at night to one in the morning, when I would walk home.

One winter, my shift ended 1:00 a.m., and the temperature was in the single digits due to a snowstorm. As I attempted to open the door at McDonald's to head home, the wind blew the snow in my face, forcing me backward.

"You aren't thinking about walking home in this weather," Carol, my manager cautioned me.

"I'm trying not to think about it, but I have no choice." She walked to the glass window, trying to have a closer look.

"You cannot walk in this weather. You will freeze to death before you get home." I collapsed in a chair near her, looking outside. *Oh my God, how am I going to get home?*

"I'll be fine," I said as my head dropped. She turned around and touched my shoulder.

"Please don't walk home in this storm." *How bad is it that strangers care more about me than my own family?* "Call your father to pick you up."

"Oh no, he will get mad if I call him at this time," I replied, shaking my head. Her mouth dropped.

"How can he get mad at you? This is an emergency."

"I know, but he doesn't care about emergencies. He already advised me to familiarize myself with all natural climates."

"I don't think he will get mad. Just call him. The worst that can happen is he will say no." I looked in her eye for a few seconds.

"Okay, I'll give it a try." She nodded and smiled. I dialed my father's number. "It's ringing. . . Hello, Papa."

"Do you know what time it's?" he growled.

"Yes, I know. I didn't want to call you, but it's snowing," I addressed in a fearful voice.

"Don't rely on me, Clesio. I told you many times. I will not always be here for you. You have to learn how to be independent." *Maybe if you would stop taking my money, I would be able to buy a car and be independent.*

"Please can you at least just pick me up today? I won't ask again."

"Clesio, there are five types of weather in the United States—snow, rain, wind, storm, and sun—and you have to get used to them. I'm not going to pick you up just because it's raining or snowing. Who is going to pick you up when you move out of my house?"

"Whoever I'm paying fifty dollars per week and fixing their entire house!" I hung up the phone. I put on a fake smile, trying to hide my anger. "Told you."

"I'm so sorry. I would drive you home, but our policy strictly prohibits managers from giving employees rides."

"Don't worry, I'll be fine." I got up. *Come on, Clesio, you will be fine.* I walked toward the door.

"Are you sure you'll be okay?"

"Yes, I'm sure. Bye, Carol. Drive safely."

"Bye. You, too, be safe out there."

Walking in the wind and blinding snow was disheartening. I had to walk backward to keep the snow from blowing in my face. Many times I had to stop, to fight the wind. After about ten minutes of stumbling in my work shoes, my feet began to hurt. I often felt my ears to make sure they were still attached because I couldn't feel them. I also had to constantly blow warm air on my hands to keep them from freezing. By the time I got home, fifty minutes felt like an eternity.

Arriving home wasn't much of a difference because we didn't have heat. We had run out of oil for the furnace, but my father hadn't bought it for two weeks. Our basement was cold even in the summertime. Sometimes in the winter, it would be colder than outside. My body began to burn and itch as it thawed. I spent hours in a tub of warm water, trying to raise my body temperature back to normal.

All the house projects were completed by late August. Suddenly, without any notice, my father evicted Neminha, Nelson, me, and Linda's children, leaving Nelson and me homeless.

CHAPTER 15

My Darkest Moments

When my father evicted us from his house, Neminha moved in with her boyfriend while Nelson and I stayed together. Since our father had charged us fifty dollars every week, in addition to repaying the deficit for my plane ticket, we never had an opportunity to save any money. As a result, we were living paycheck to paycheck.

Nelson and I managed to rent a basement apartment within walking distance from my father's house. The expenses were more than we could afford. Our combined $2,040 monthly income was insufficient to pay the $880 for rent, the groceries, and household, car, and personal expenses, as well as trying to help our mothers in Cape Verde. In order to meet these expenses, I had to drop out of high school to work overtime. My paycheck was so small that working overtime really didn't make any difference. Because math never compromises, it was impossible to cover all our expenses.

We fell two months behind in our rent. Many times, I would be scared to go home because I couldn't face the landlord. I would search around the house to see when the landlord wasn't outside so I could dash inside unseen. The situation grew worse every day; the landlord left warning notes on our door, stating that we had one month to pay the overdue rent or vacate the apartment. Unfortunately, at this exact time, my mother had an emergency, requiring my immediate financial support. So though I only had about $160 in my checking account, I withdrew $200 to send to her. This resulted in more than $300 in overdraft fees. Soon after, my car insurance company sent me a cancelation note because I was unable to keep up with my premiums.

My car insurance cancelation turned into more than a thousand dollars of parking tickets. The police would give me tickets for parking an uninsured vehicle on a public road and then call their friends to ticket me again—they would give me two to three tickets every day. A month later, they towed my vehicle, requiring me to pay the full amount of parking tickets in addition to the $250 tow fee. Since I couldn't afford to pay to claim my vehicle, they charged me an extra $20 per day.

I became overwhelmed with my responsibilities. My head would hurt, and the veins in my forehead would pop out. Many times I feared that the police were going to arrest me for not paying my car bills. I wouldn't sleep at night because I knew it was only a matter of time before the landlord evicted us. I would also think about how I would react in case of an emergency since I didn't have any money. How would I buy clothing or do my laundry? How would I eat as a homeless person? And where would I sleep?

There were no answers. At this moment, I saw no way out, and I even considered taking drugs as a way of escaping my problems. I had heard many people talk about how drugs would take them out of this world and help them forget about problems. But I realized that drugs weren't the solution to my problems because I wanted a permanent solution, not just a few hours. As a result, I constantly forced myself to face reality and try not to make the situation worse. I understood the consequences of taking drugs, and I knew its side effects were more costly and more life threatening than my problems alone.

I suffered, hopeless. My purpose for living diminished with every day. It was too painful to live—I lost sense of direction. I lost myself. And I lost the meaning of life. I couldn't take it anymore, especially when bad things were happening too fast at the same time. My girlfriend, who was the only person to keep me distracted from my problems, had just broken up with me. And now I lost connection with the world—no one to talk to and no one to cry with. My brother was dealing with his own problems, so he was almost never home.

I was a mental and emotional wreck. One day, I just wanted the pain to go away and, for once, to rest in peace. So I decided to commit suicide. I went to the nearest pharmacy, bought a bottle of pills for headaches, ran home, and swallowed more than twenty capsules. I began to cry inconsolably. *Mommy, I'm so sorry. I'm so sorry. I don't know what else to do. I tried so hard, but it's too much for me to handle. I can't take this pain anymore. Why do I always have to suffer? I'm much of a failure. I'm sorry, Grandma. I'm so sorry for disappointing you.*

Still crying on my bed, I grabbed my blanket, covered myself, closed my eyes, and waited for my life to end. As I lay there, I kept thinking about how devastated my life had been, when remembered about the vow I made to myself—fight until the end in honor of the five-year-boy. Plus I couldn't allow a difficult moment to determine me. *I'm stronger than this. I'm going to fight until the end, not end it to escape the fight.* Since I had overcome all my obstacles since age five, I realized could overcome anything in my life. The five-year-old who sacrificed day and night wouldn't want to see this twenty-year-old give up now. I needed to be strong not only for myself but for my mother as well. *If I die, who will take care of my mother? Clesio, you cannot die now. What about your dreams? The day must come when your mother can hug you and whisper in your ear that she is proud of you.*

I quickly jumped out of the bed. Shaking, I began searching for my phone to call 911. My heart was beating at an increasing rate as the clock ticked. I patted my pocket and looked on the bed for my phone. Where could it be? *Crap, crap, where is the stupid phone!*

From bended knee, I groveled around the room and under the bed, desperately trying to locate it, but still no phone. Rushing through, I hit my head on one of the supporting pillars as I turned to inspect in the kitchen. After about two minutes, I kicked the trash can near the stove out of frustration. "Where is the stupid phone?" I yelled. Aware of my trembling knees, I felt my blood vessel throb from time to time.

Trying to stay focused, I ran back to the bedroom, frantic to find my phone. Feeling dizzy, I rummaged my bed, under the bed, myself, and the closet. Still no phone. *It has to be here somewhere.* My steps began to feel heavier, and my vision began to blur. *Clesio, stay calm. When was the last time you used the phone?* Finally, I looked under my pillow . . . and it was there.

Panicking, I tried entering Clefogocv#19 as password into my BlackBerry, but my hands were too shaky, causing me to fail three out of four attempts. I sat on the bed and took a deep breath. *Clesio, calm down, calm down. You can't enter the last attempt incorrectly.* I look another deep breath and slowly entered the password, one character at a time, and it unlocked.

Suddenly I couldn't remember what I was supposed to be doing now that my phone was unlocked. I stared at the screen, my eyes going in and out of focus. Damn, what was it? I shook my head a little bit, but my thoughts kept drifting in and out. Bills, money, pills, money. Pills! Nothing. I paced around, using the pillars as a support so I wouldn't fall. *I know I'm supposed to be doing something. What is it?* I sat back on bed, pulling my hair with both hands as I tried to remember. Then I heard a siren rushing nearby. *Oh yeah, 911.* I dialed 911.

An ambulance arrived shortly after and I was rushed to the emergency room. I could hear the siren and knew they were rushing me to the hospital. I dreaded my possibility of surviving.

Upon our arrival, the paramedics rushed me to the emergency room, and I could heard doctors yelling, "Hurry, hurry, we don't have much time."

"Doctor, am I going to die?" I asked in a fearful voice. The doctors and the paramedics looked at each other.

"There is no way for us to know right now," one of the doctors said as she pulled the bed cart into the emergency room. *God, please don't let me die.*

"Listen, I'm going to give you an emetic to help clean the pills out of your system."

"So, I'm not going to die?" she reached down and rubbed the back of my hands.

"We won't know until midnight. I have to be honest with you. You swallowed plenty of pills, so there is a possibility of a negative outcome. But we will do our best to treat you," she delivered, without a shred of confidence in her voice. She left, but she kept checking on me regularly.

Waiting for the result was painful and torturous. The clock hands seemed as if they weren't moving. Every time, I felt something unusual, my heart would beat rapidly, my feet would get cold, and the saliva would stick in my throat. In fact, because I was scared, I felt something weird throughout the entire time. I kept feeling my pulse every minute to assure myself I was still alive.

Nelson came to visit me immediately after he learned what I had done.

"How are you?" Nelson gave me a casual greeting.

"Fine, I guess," I answered, panicking, but I tried to look confident.

"What happened?"

"Nelson, can we please not talk about this now?"

"Sure. What do you want to talk about?"

"That's your job. Isn't that what a big brother is for? To comfort me."

"Are you hungry? Do you want a cheeseburger?"

"So, this is what it takes to get a free sandwich. No, I'm not hungry, but thank you for offering."

"Let me go outside to call Papa, and I will be right back."

"Okay."

About ten minutes later, Nelson returned. His head dropped, forehead creased, and mouth turned down.

"What happened? What did he say?" I investigated, worried.

"He isn't coming. He said he has to do a task for Linda."

"Wow. Clearly a task is more important than me." *What is the use of a father? He doesn't show me a friendship, he doesn't help me moneywise, and he isn't even here when I need him the most.*

Nelson and I waited until about midnight, when the doctor approached with a file in her hands. As she walked toward me, I felt myself on the verge of total panic.

"Good news," the doctor said, smiling. *Thank you, God, for keeping me safe.* "I'm going to give you some medication that will continue to help clean out your system, and then you will be ready to go home."

"Nelson, you hear that? I'm going home." He smiled.

A week after I returned home from the hospital, the landlord evicted us from the basement and requested us to pay the debt within sixty days, or he would take us to court. Since Nelson and I didn't have a place to go, we decided that it would be best for us to go on our separate ways. After the eviction, we barely saw each other because my phone service was cancelled. We would be together only when we were scheduled to work on the same day.

I rented a unit from U-Haul to store my belongings. I would work during the day and during the night searched for a safe street to sleep in.

I never wanted night to come because my heart would drop every time I remembered I had nowhere to sleep. Sometimes, I would cry even when trying not to; the tears would just slip and roll down my face. Many times, I would wish I could go on top of a high mountain and scream as loud as I could.

On my first night as a homeless person, I slept in a park near a soccer field. I scanned the area to find a quiet and safe place. While surveying the area, I saw a group of guys in their early twenties, wearing hoodies. I could hear them swearing and laughing. I attempted to avoid them, but two approached me regardless. One was wearing a black sweater, jeans, and black sneakers. The other was wearing a dark brown jacket, jeans, and Timberlake boots.

"Hey you!" the person with the black sweater yelled as he strolled toward me. His friend followed. Immediately I began to shake, and I could feel dread building in my throat, heart, and shoulders.

Keep cool, keep cool, and don't show them you are scared.

"Hey, what's up?" I asked, praying that they wouldn't detect how scared I was. They suddenly looked at each other and began laughing as though I had said something funny. "Hey, you look familiar. Do you go to school around this area?" I asked the person in black, hoping it would make a positive impression.

"Naaah, kid, you are mistaken. I don't go to school," he replied as he pulled his pants up.

The person with the brown jacket moved and stood behind me. The leader in black reached into his pocket while he threw me a smile over his shoulder.

"Do you go to school?" I asked the person in the brown jacket as I turned toward him to avoid having him behind me.

"Enough with the twenty questions!" he snapped.

"Okay, you don't have to yell, you know," I stressed, smiling, trying to maintain my confidence. *Please don't take it in the wrong way*, I prayed.

"Are you trying to be cute, kid?" he shot back.

"So, I'm guessing you are saying I'm *not* cute. That hurts."

"Oh, I like this kid!" the person in black interfered.

"See that, I like you too," I responded as I raised my hand to give him a high five. Then the rest of the group came and surrounded me.

Okay, now I'm a dead man.

"What are you doing here, kid?" one of them asked in an intimidating voice. My knees and legs were still shaking, and I froze for a moment. The words wouldn't come out of my mouth. Struggling to fight the fear, I cleared my throat, took a step closer to him, and opened my body so I could appear comfortable.

"Just walking around to enjoy the view. Thank you for asking." All of them looked at each other fascinated, and amazed that I was facing them fearlessly. At least, they thought so. "Nice soccer field, isn't it?" They nodded.

"Don't you know it's dangerous walking alone around here?" the person in black cautioned me.

"What do you mean dangerous?" I asked, pretending that I didn't know what he was talking about.

"Dude, we were about to kick your ass and rob you."

"Really? Wow, thanks for not doing that and thank you for being honest with me. From now on, I will not walk here alone again." Then, I shook everyone's hand and left.

I walked a big loop, pretending I was leaving, and hid behind a wall and waited for them to leave. While waiting, I kept calming myself, realizing how lucky I was to be still breathing. After they left, I climbed a fence, and as I attempted to jump to the next side, my shirt got stuck in the fence, causing me to land hard on my stomach. I got up, feeling a sharp pain and bent over slightly, holding my stomach. *Damn, how can my night be any worse?*

Resisting the pain, I hunched over and made it to a dark area between a few trees. Then I knelt down to clear the area to make a bed, and then I walked around to collect leaves and plants to use as a cushion.

The leaves and plants irritated my skin and caused it to itch throughout the night, producing bumps all over my body. Besides itching, the hard ground was covered with small rocks, making it extremely uncomfortable to sleep.

About midnight, a cold April rain started to fall. I didn't even have appropriate clothing for rain. The wind kept blowing cold, salty water on my face and body, causing my skin to wrinkle. Often I had to take my shirt off, wring out the water, and wear it again. By the time it was near morning, I could barely feel my ears, and I had to constantly blow warm air on my hands.

Fighting to stay strong, I kept wiping tears from my eyes. At that moment, I wished I could go back to Cape Verde. *Why do I have to suffer wherever I go? Why doesn't anyone love me? Why won't anyone care about me? I've never done anything wrong, so why am I being punished? Will I ever have a better life? Or even have a normal life? Will I ever be loved?*

Clesio, think positive. You are strong. Stay strong. You will survive. You are strong. You are strong. You will survive. I chanted in my head, trying to convince myself to stay strong.

****

After being homeless for weeks, my friend Jose learned about my situation and offered me a place to sleep in at his parents' (Mindela and Manuel) house, where Jose's three siblings also lived. Even though there was no extra room, Jose's parents welcomed me until I could find a place of my own.

For about two weeks, I would sleep at Jose's parents' house, except when I worked late nights. Then I would sleep outside to avoid waking them up at 2:00 a.m.

Even with a place to sleep sometimes, I was still distressed, worried that I may overstay my welcome before I became financially stable. When I was around people, they would talk and laugh, but I would be too distracted, thinking about my abhorrent situation. Many times, when they looked at me, I would give them a fake smile, pretending I knew what they were talking about. Even when I was around people, I was alone.

CHAPTER 16

Aunt Sabel

A miracle phone call. One day as I was running to work in my McDonalds' uniform—a red buttoned-up shirt, a black pants, black dressing shoes, and a topless hat—I ran by a girl who was walking in the opposite direction.

"Clesio?" she called, unsure.

Still running, I turned my head, but I didn't recognize the person. I slowly halted and walked toward her. "Yeah?"

"You are so big. I almost didn't recognize you." She met me a halfway, extending her arms to hug me. I awkwardly hugged her back, still trying to figure out how she knew my name. She delicately released, and she could read my puzzled face. "You don't remember me, do you?" I shook my head, wide-eyed. "It's me, Antonia. We used to be neighbors back when you lived with your grandmother in Campana. I used to steal your toys, remember?"

"Oh my God, I remember now. You used to give you piggy back rides."

"Yes! yes!" Her face lit up.

"When did you come to the United States?"

"About seven months ago."

"Nice, how do you like America?" I inquired, eager for her impression.

"Too cold, but I like it. I just miss my family back home. What about you?"

"Oh, I can't complain."

"I saw your aunt three months ago."

"Which one?"

"The one who lives near a Laundromat. But I think she moved. I forget her name."

"From my mother side?"

"Yeah, she visited a lot when we were younger."

"Oh, Sabel."

"Yup, Sabel."

"Do you have her phone number because I've been trying to reach her?"

"I do actually. And here, take mine too."

I instantly had goose bumps and as she read the number to me, my heart felt relieved. Could this be the end of my nightmare? Was it a coincidence I ran into her or was it meant to be? My lips unconsciously stretched into a big smile.

"I've to go now because I'm running late for work, but it was nice seeing you again after all these years." I inched closer and hugged her for a final goodbye.

"It was good seeing you, too, and you have my number now. Please don't be a stranger." She waved goodbye as I gradually stepped backward.

Later that day I asked my manager to allow me to leave at 9:00 p.m. instead of 12:00 a.m. so I could arrive at Joao's parents' house before they fall asleep, to call Sabel. With my supervisor permission, I left ten minutes to nine and speeded home.

I arrived at Joao's at about 9:40 p.m. and rang the doorbell. I placed both of my hands against the wall, facing down, trying to catch my breath. *I hope someone is here.*

"Are the police chasing you?" Joao asked, smiling as he opened the door.

"Yeah, the police are after me," I responded sarcastically.

"Then you can't come in." He attempted to close the door in my face, but I stuck my foot in it.

"Come on, dude. I'm out of breath because I ran here. I need to make an important call."

"Oh, who is she? Who is she?" he asked, excited.

"My aunt. I'm calling her to ask if she'll let me stay with her." We stepped into the kitchen and sat at the table. "Where is everybody?"

"They're all out somewhere."

"Oh, thanks, that was very helpful. Can I use the phone in your room?"

"Sure."

"And for God's sake, don't come into your room until I'm done. This is serious, so no joking." We laughed. I went to his room and dialed the digits.

"Hello, Sabel? I'm Clesio," I said.

"Oh, hi. How have you been?" Sabel replied. "Haven't seen you in a long time."

"I know. I've been having some problems lately," I disclosed, halting.

"Why? What is wrong?"

"That's why I'm calling. My father evicted me from his house, and I've been homeless for almost a month. I-I." I hesitated over the next words. My body temperature rose, along with my pulse. I wiped my sweaty forehead with a white T-shirt before attempting again. "I don't have anywhere to go, so I was wondering if it is possible to stay with you for a couple of days."

"Why did your father evict you?"

"I still don't know."

"I don't understand this at all. When you first came to the United States, I asked him if you could stay with me, but he refused." Her voice was raised in frustration.

"When we first arrived here, he still needed me to renovate his house, and now that the house is finished, he doesn't need me anymore." I paused. "Wait, did you say you asked him if I could live with you?"

"Yes, but he refused." I felt a cold breeze rushing down my spine. *The bastard.*

"He never told me anything."

"Of course he wouldn't say anything. Anyways, my house is a little crowded right now. My son Sandro and my daughter Sandra just emigrated from Cape Verde, and they are living with me now. But we are family. You can come, and we can all sleep together." Tears instantly filled my eyes. This was the first time I had ever been called "family" and the first time to hear "we could all be together."

"Thank you very much. I don't even know what to say."

"Don't say anything. Are you coming right now?" I wiped the tears from my face and cleared my throat.

"Yes."

"Do you know where I live? We moved to a new house. It's behind your father's old house."

"Okay, thank you so much. I will call you when I'm near." *I hope Joao allows me to borrow his cell phone.*

"Okay, see you soon."

From the moment of that phone call, I felt as if the whole world had been removed from my shoulders. No more worries about where to sleep. No more worries about not making it the next day. And no more worries about my next meal.

I rushed to my aunt. Sabel, in her middle forties, had a loving motherly nature. Sabel was the kind of person who would feed you and stay hungry herself just like my mother. If she got on your case, it meant she cared for you.

Sabel greeted me at the door.

"Come in!" Sabel invited, hugging me. She then slowly released me.

As I walked into the living room, my mouth dropped. I couldn't believe my eyes. Three pieces of a large white leather sectional couch were arranged around a glass-topped coffee table. To the left of the couch was a matching desk with a Mac computer. A large plasma television hung on a soft cocoa brown wall. White and brown patterned drapes accented the color of the walls. A white glass-topped table with four ladder-back chairs created a dining area in the open space of the living room. Next to this area, I could see in the kitchen a huge silver refrigerator and a matching microwave, a dishwasher, a stove, and a sink. I had never seen so many modern appliances in one place. A brown marble-topped breakfast island with tall stools created a boundary between the kitchen and the living room.

Sandro, a slim nineteen-year-old with curly black hair, was sitting at the computer, while Sandra, twenty-four-year-old, friendly and caring like her mother, was standing in the kitchen. Sandro walked up to me and gave me a handshake. Then I made my way to the kitchen and hugged Sandra.

"Where have you been? I missed you," Sandra greeted me with excitement.

"I've been everywhere. I miss you, too. This house is beautiful," I said, amazed.

"Thanks," Sabel responded proudly as she pulled a high stool from the kitchen for me. Sandra filled my plate with rice and chicken and other vegetables, while Sabel poured orange juice into my glass.

"Where are Kevin and Keyla?"

"They're in their rooms," Sabel responded, pointing to a bedroom facing the kitchen and then to another bedroom down the hall. "You grew up so fast. I still remember you crawling at my mother's house." Sandra and I glanced at each other, smiling.

After I had eaten my fill, I went to Keyla's room to say hi. Keyla, who appreciated the beauty of art and books, was skinny. Even though she was thirteen years old, most people would assume she was years younger by her appearance. She was about five foot four, with long curly brown hair, brown eyes, and a small smile. Her personality could be easily misunderstood because she did not like to interact with anyone. She would come from school and go straight to her room.

Later Sabel gave me a tour of the house. She led me down a hallway to show me Sandra's and her rooms on the left and two bathrooms on the right. The second bathroom faced Sandro and Kevin's room. To the right of the back door were a washing machine and a dryer.

"When you're ready, you can take a shower in the larger bathroom." She pointed to the bathroom facing the boys' room after the tour. She then walked to the closet in the bathroom, grabbed a clean towel, and handed it to me. "You can have it."

"Oh, thank you."

"There are new toothbrushes. Grab one."

"Okay." *Oh my God, this place is like a store.*

"I'm going to bed because I have to work early in the morning. I will talk to you tomorrow after work."

"Okay."

I sang in the bathtub as I was taking my shower.

After the shower, I stood in front of the mirror and thought how lucky I was to find a home and someone who actually cared about me. I took a deep breath, wrapped in my new towel, and stepped into Sandro and Kevin's bedroom.

"I have some extra clothing here. If you want, you can have them," Sandro offered, pulling jeans, T-shirts, and sweaters out of his drawer.

"Sure, I ran out of clothing a couple of days ago."

"Hi, Kevin, how are you? You're so big now."

Kevin, adorable, was nine years old. He had black hair and dark eyes.

"Hi," Kevin said, lifting himself up to sit on the bed.

"Do you remember me?"

"A little bit. You visited our old house when you first came to the United States, right?"

"Yes. Once. And you were so little." He smiled.

"My mother talks about you a lot. Why haven't you visited for such a long time?" I took another deep breath.

"Because I lost contact."

I returned to the bathroom and closed the door to change into my new clothing. Kevin followed and stood immediately outside the door.

"Are you going to live with us?" he asked, leaning against the door.

"Yeah, for a couple of days."

"Why not forever?"

I finished dressing before answering and slowly opened the door, expecting him to be leaning against it.

"Because there isn't enough space for me," I answered, wrapping my arm around his shoulders and walking with him to the room.

"You can sleep in my bed with me. I don't kick while I sleep." I smiled.

"Thank you very much, you're very sweet, but I will sleep on the couch so you can sleep more comfortably." I rubbed his head.

"Clesio, if you want to sleep on my bed, you can. I don't mind sleeping on the couch," Sandro offered.

"No, it's fine. I will take the couch. I love couches." We laughed.

"Are you sure?" he insisted.

"Yeah, I'm sure."

"Okay, here are the blankets and a pillow. Let me know if you need anything else."

"Thanks."

And thus began my first comfortable night in a long time.

The next day, when Sabel returned home from work, Keyla, Kevin, and I were watching television in the living room. Sandra and Sandro had just left for work.

"How you guys doing?" Sabel asked, walking toward us. "Have you eaten?"

"Yes, Sandra cooked lunch," I answered. She kissed Keyla and Kevin on the forehead.

"Clesio, can I please talk to you?" My heart dropped instantly.

Oh no, please don't kick me out of this beautiful house.

"Sure," I responded, fearful. I followed her to her room.

"Please close the door," she requested.

Yeah, I guess this is it. I should go pack. Oh wait, I don't have anything to pack.

"You can sit here." She slid over and pointed to the bed, indicating for me to sit next to her. "Clesio, I want to talk to you because if you are going to stay here, you should know a few house rules."

Oh thank God, she isn't evicting me.

"Okay, that's fair enough."

"As you can see, I have two children in the house, so I don't like to set bad examples for them. When you plan to bring friends, please make sure you let me know in advance. And of course, no alcohol or drugs are allowed."

"Okay, that's no problem. I don't smoke or drink, and I don't have that many friends anyway."

"I will make you a copy of the house key. And for as long as you are in school, you don't have to worry about paying rent or anything else. I will provide everything, and make sure you save your money and help your mother in Cape Verde."

This can't be real. I must be dreaming.

"I don't know what to say." She leaned and hugged me.

"You don't have to say anything. That's what family is for. I'm sure you've been through a lot."

"That's what *some* families are for."

She laughed. She released me slowly, and we went to the kitchen.

After living with my aunt Sable for a year, all her children considered me their brother. Even thirteen-year-old Keyla, who barely spoke with anyone at the house, became my best friend. The only time she ever laughed was when I was home. Kevin, in fact, asked Keyla why she only laughed when I was home. She shrugged with a small giggle and went back to her room.

Kevin and Keyla never really noticed when Sabel, Sandra, or Sandro left or arrived home. But every time I attempted to go somewhere, they would ask where I was going, and they would walk me to the door.

Keyla would stay in her room all day, but as soon as she heard my voice, she would run out, smiling.

"Where have you been?" Keyla would ask.

"I went to a meeting, Mommy."

"How many times, have I told you not to leave home without my permission?"

"Sorry, I promise it will not happen again."

"That sounds familiar, doesn't it?"

"Yes, it does," I agreed, nodding. I hugged her.

Kevin came out of his room with his arm opened and joined the group hug.

"Where have you been?" he asked. I could feel he wasn't happy with my absence.

"I went to a meeting, Daddy."

"How can I be your daddy if you are older than me?" he quizzed, laughing.

I thought how ironic it was that even though they were just kids, their concerns were as genuine as that of loving parents.

CHAPTER 17

Finding Love

Growing up, love seemed so easy to me. People love one another, move in together, and raise their family. Since I spent the majority of my life working and dealing with problems, I didn't have much time understanding the fundamental concept of love. Nevertheless, I developed a crush on a girl named Edna in Cape Verde, whom I never had the chance or courage to talk to. Edna had a light skin color and a long curly hair, which extended bellow her shoulders. Her brown eyes, along with her adorable smile and taste for fashion, always invited comfort. Though she wore a serious look on her face, she enjoyed humor, music, and movies.

It wasn't until 2005, when this young woman came to the United States, that a window of opportunity opened. But her father's over-protectiveness and my father's demands stalled this process for a while.

With Edna, an opportunity doesn't necessarily guarantee a relationship. When I was able to speak with her, she quickly clarified that she wasn't interested in dating.

One day, at Saint Peter's while doing my homework, I noticed Edna being given a tour of the program by a staff member. I glared at her, surprised with her presence. My heart elevated instantly. I spontaneously cracked my knuckles and tapped my fingers on the table where I was doing my homework, along with my friends. My friends craned their heads and threw me funky looks. I threw them a half-creepy smile in return, tying to act natural. *I should go say hi. Or maybe not. What if she just ignores me? I'll look stupid in front of everybody. But this could be an ice breaker to talk to her. Damn, Clesio. Think. Think! You know what? Don't think. Just go.* Nervously, I stood up half way but sat right back, lacking courage. I was a bundle of nerves.

"Clesio, are you okay?" Placido who was also sitting at the table, reading, asked with a concerned face.

"Yes, I'm okay. Just read your book." I re-grew my courage and stood up again, but my legs refused to work. I eventually trudged toward her. "Hey, how are you? What are you doing here?" I greeted her, excited.

"I enrolled here to improve my English," Edna answered, turning her head, surveying around curiously.

"I come here, too," I informed her, smiling.

"Oh, nice." Without much attention, she resumed with her tour.

Edna attended Saint Peter regularly, but I showed up whenever I was available. Since I barely have time to go to Saint Peter, I tried to take advantage of my limited window of opportunity. Being allowed to walk her home was my greatest opportunity, though it didn't ensure anything beyond walking. She periodically reminded me that she wasn't interested in a relationship.

About five months after Edna's enrollment, I walked in late and sat down next to her at her table.

"Hi." *Keep it short and sweet.*

"Hey," Edna replied.

"How are you?" I asked, trying to continue a conversation.

"I'm good. How are you?"

"Other than my heart speeding at two hundred miles per hour, I'm good."

"Why is your heart speeding?"

"Well, It's hard to tell. It was fine before I saw you, but as soon I set my eyes on you, it automatically began speeding."

"Clesio, as I told you, I am not interested in a relationship. I'm sorry."

"No, no, there is nothing to be sorry for. I'm going to leave you alone."

"I have a lot of homework to do." She got up and sat at a different table.

Even though she didn't give me any hope, I didn't want to give her up. She was the only girl I ever developed feelings for. She was the only one who could make my heart skip a beat or two. I wanted to win her over without becoming annoying, a creep, or a stalker. As a result, I devoted my leisure, learning how to become a romantic expert so I could steal her heart.

Toward this goal, I spent a lot of time with Djedje, my father's brother-in-law, because I admired his relationship with this wife. Every time, I saw them together, they would tease and flirt with each other, and not once did I ever see them get mad at one another. One day, they came to my father's house for a visit.

"Djedje, can I please talk to you?" I asked.

"Sure, what's up?"

"I mean in private. This is too personal." I took Djedje to my room in the basement. He sat on the bed while I stood next to it. "I chose to talk to you because as you probably know, I admire your relationship—you and your wife are very friendly, and you guys never argue like a lot of couples I know. How do you maintain much a beautiful relationship?"

"First, you have to understand what a relationship takes. A relationship requires honesty, commitment, responsibility, understanding, patience, and, most importantly, forgiveness. You have to internalize each one of these elements. You also have to always remember that a relationship involves two different people. What may seem okay in her eyes may not always seem okay to you, and vice versa. Second, you have to know what your intentions are. Do you want a committed relationship, or do you just want to chill?" I took note as he explained.

"I want a committed relationship. I really like this girl, Edna, but she isn't interested."

"If you really like her, you have to work hard."

"How?"

"You have to make yourself unique. Anyone can ask a girl out, but not everyone is a gentleman. Stop focusing on the relationship. Focus on being her best friend. Be the one whom she shares her problems with. Always be there for her as a friend, not as a boyfriend. Don't ask her to fall in love with you. Make her fall in love with you. Buy her flowers occasionally and mail sweet letters to her address. When you take her out, hold doors for her. Make her feel special."

I nodded while writing down his tips. "I honestly thought a relationship was way easier than this. But I think I can do that. Oh, wait, what if I forget to hold the door?"

"Don't worry about that. Just practice." He got up and tapped on my shoulder. "Clesio, you're a nice guy. You need to show this girl that. Just be yourself."

"I'm not sure being myself is a good idea. But all right I'll try it."

"Don't be hard on yourself. You will be fine."

"Thank you. I feel much better now."

"Anytime. I will always be here for you."

"Djedje?" someone called him from upstairs.

"Let me go. You-know-who is calling, but we will talk some more."

"I know, she misses you already. Yeah, I will keep you posted. Can you please send Nelson down here?"

About two minutes later, Nelson came downstairs, running.

"What's up?" he asked, out of breath.

"Were police chasing you?"

"Ha-ha, very funny." He entered the bedroom and dropped himself abruptly on the bed. "Why did you call me? Do you have anything for me?"

"Well, no. But I need you to be my date for a couple of days." Immediately he attempted to walk out. I ran, grabbed his hand, and pulled him back into the room. "Wait, wait!"

"Clesio, that's not how you ask people out. No wonder you are single. First, you don't use the word *need* when you ask people on a date, and secondly, you don't ask people out just for a couple of dates. At least not me. It's either forever or never," he challenged, fighting not to laugh.

"Good point. But can we please get serious here?"

"Okay, but I should warn you. You are a bad date."

"That's why I need to practice. I need you to be my date so I can practice." His eyebrows rose. "Wait a minute! What you do mean I'm a bad date? How do you know?"

"Just forget it. But yeah, I will be your date. Oh, this is going to be fun." His bug-eyed expression indicated he was going to give me a hard time.

"I'm regretting this already."

"Come on, it's going to be fun."

"Anyways. For now, when we go out, I will hold the door for you, be nice to you, and be very understanding. Just to be clear, no flowers, no holding hands, and no paying for anything, whatsoever."

"Oh man, you take all the fun out of it."

I spent a year and a half implementing what I had learned to win Edna's heart. I held the door for her, sent her roses, and, most importantly, became her best friend. I was the person she disclosed her troubles with. I became an essential part of her life. She unintentionally began developing feelings for me.

On January 9, 2007, I went to Saint Peter's afterschool program, ready to ask Edna out on a date. This time, I reported later than normal. By the time I arrived, students had just finished studying, so they were playing games before they went home. Some students were playing cards or foosball, while others were playing pool.

I decided to play pool with my friends Roberto, Morais, and my cousin Placido, all the while keeping an eye on when Edna would leave.

"You look distracted today." Placido noticed.

"Nah, I'm not distracted at all." *I hope he doesn't learn about my plan.* "What makes you think I'm distracted?" I spoke as though I didn't know what he was talking about.

He paused, lining up a shot, and looked straight at me.

"You're kidding me, right? Your mind is elsewhere. It's like your body is here but your mind is on the moon."

"Yeah, Clesio, you're usually so annoying about the rules, but today you aren't even paying attention. No offense," Roberto said.

"No, no, none taken." I looked at my watch and turned my head toward the table where Edna was sitting.

"See, you did it again," Placido insisted.

"Did what?" I played innocent again.

"For half an hour, you've been looking at your watch and then over there." Everyone around the pool table stopped and stared at me.

"You know, I've a curfew, so I have to make sure I go home on time," I lied.

Ultimately Edna passed by us, waving goodbye. I waited with bated breath. *How am I going to get out of here without making a scene?*

"Oh, look at the time. It's my curfew, time to go."

"I thought your curfew was 9:00 p.m."

"Yeah, it was, but my father reduced it to 8:00 p.m., so I have to leave now." *I think he bought it.* I quickly put on my sweater and strode until I was out of view, and then I stormed out. *Where is she? She cannot be that far.*

At the exit, I spotted Edna crossing the street. *Damn, it's cold. I need to learn how to bring a jacket with me.*

"Hey!" I yelled as I ran toward her. She turned her head towards my voice after she successfully crossed the street. "Can I please talk to you?" I proposed, trying to catch my breath.

"Talk about what?" she waited for me to cross the street.

"Something I wanted to tell you for a year and a half now. I just want you to listen because I cannot go one more day without telling you how I feel about you. My heart just can't take it anymore."

"Okay, come with me. I am going to show you somewhere." Edna smiled.

I stopped a few feet away from her. *Where is this girl taking me?*

"I hope the somewhere isn't your father's house because I'm too young to die." Her lips stretched into a smile.

"Are you scared to die? If you want me to listen to you, you have to trust me," she uttered softly as her eyebrows rose. I couldn't read her enigma smile.

"Hell yeah, I'm scared to die, but only when I'm not with you."

"You are too much."

"Seriously, should I call my family to say goodbye?" She laughed.

We walked about three minutes up a hill to a park.

"Look, see the park over there? From now on, I want it to be our park. It can be our place to hang out and talk since we can't talk anywhere else without interruptions."

I instantly stopped in disbelief and became emotional. I had goose bumps because those were the most beautiful words I had ever heard in my life. *Clesio, don't cry, don't cry.* I turned my face away, trying to conceal my feelings.

"I don't know what to say."

"You don't need to say anything."

I held her hand, walked to a bench, and we sat down. It was dark, but a few light poles illuminated the park. Several houses hidden behind trees surrounded the park, which enhanced our privacy. To our left was a playground setting, whereas to our right, down a hill, was a soccer/baseball field. The weather was cold with the wind probably at nine miles per hour.

My lower eyelids rose to form crescent shape as I tried to think about something to break the awkward silence. But I couldn't articulate my cluttered thoughts before she turned and threw me a sincere smile.

"Are you cold?" she asked.

"No, no," I answered with a straight face. "Are you?"

"Yeah, a little bit."

Hesitating, I slid and hugged her sideways. She leaned her head on my shoulder. The smell of her hair invited comfort, while her cologne just melted my heart away.

"Don't worry, I will keep you warm."

"Thanks." She raised her head and looked into my eyes. "So, what do you want to tell me?"

"Damn, I was hoping you would forget." I took a deep breath and slowly exhale. "Here it goes," I said with an inaudible voice. "As you already know, I'm crazy about you. Edna, I know you aren't interested in a relationship, but please understand that I have spent a year and a half trying to keep you off my mind. But I can't stop thinking about you, not even for a minute." I gently grabbed her chin and slowly raised it so our eyes were level. "I don't know what else to do."

"Clesio, I know what you mean. I can't stop thinking about you either." She leaned and wrapped her hands around me. "You made it really hard, not to fall for you," she added. *Am I dreaming? Is this real? It must be true because I'm very cold.*

A few minutes later, she stood up. "Are you sure you're not cold?" she asked as though she already knew the answer.

"Of course I'm not. My skin is coldproof." She shook her head, wide-eyed. I got up and hugged her from behind.

"I have a confession to make. I-I . . ." She hesitated. *Oh no, don't tell me you have a boyfriend*. Nervously, I turned her around.

"What is it?" I worried, reaching for her hand. "You can count on me. No matter what, I will be here to support you." I filled in during her pause.

"I never had a boyfriend before." She looked into my eyes. "You know what this means? It means I don't know how to ki—" I interrupted her by pulling her closer toward my body and kissed her. "Kiss," she added after the kiss.

I grabbed her chin and slightly pulled it up.

"You don't have to know. I'll teach you."

We slowly perambulated the park, holding hands.

"By the way, nice try, pretending you aren't cold," she revealed after we kissed goodbye.

****

Our relationship was beautiful; we never had an argument with each other, even when we encountered conflicts. We always resolved our differences in a respectful manner, taking into account each other's feelings. We barely had disagreements because we focused more on the positive. We would play and joke with each other. Many people, in fact, admired our relationship; her family even mentioned that we were an example of how a relationship should be.

While many people were impressed with our relationship, some were jealous, especially her friends. Some of Edna's friends resented the fact that I was always there for her, bringing and picking her up from school and work, while their boyfriends wouldn't even pick them up after work. They were jealous because for no special reason, I would buy flowers and bring them to Edna either at school or at work.

Not surprisingly, Edna's friends decided to tear us apart. They told Edna I was cheating on her, while telling me that Edna had been talking to a guy at school. Slowly our relationship fell apart. Edna stopped calling me, and when I would call her, she wouldn't answer, or if she did, she would quickly make excuses to get off the phone. *Something isn't right.*

On June 14, 2008, a year and five months after we had begun dating, Edna asked me to meet her at our park. From the way she spoke over the phone, I knew this would be our last meeting. I rushed to the park, and from a distance, I saw her sitting at the same bench from our first day, with her head dropped.

"Clesio, we can't do this anymore," she expressed after I sat next to her. "We're falling apart, and it's too painful. Every day, I hear more stories at school." I could sense the sadness and the frustration in her voice.

"Edna, we can't let people destroy us. We're strong together."

"I'm only seventeen. I'm not ready to deal with all this drama. It's too much, and it's interfering with school. If it's meant to be, maybe one day we'll retry, but for now, I just want to focus on school." My blood ran cold. My heart felt as if someone had punched a harp stick through it. I tried to gather my courage to understand. Besides, her happiness was my number one mission.

"Can we at least be friends?"

"Sure, we can always be friends."

"I'm going to miss you."

"I'm going to miss you too."

She wiped her tears and hugged me. She then released me, took a deep breath, and she slowly walked away. As she vanished in the distance everything went black. Nothing mattered anymore. During my burdensome days, she was the only one who could distract me, and now she was gone.

Yet, I cared too much to abstain from the relationship, especially since the decision to break up was against her will. During the separation, I remained treating her in the same manner as a boyfriend, proving I would always care for her, despite the estrangement. I continued to buy her a Valentine's gift every year, to drive her to and from school and work, and to be there when she needed someone to talk to. Admitting my desire to restore our relationship, I invested time and energy without any intention to win her back.

Though she eventually revealed some obvious signs, indicating her interest, she did her best to suppress her feelings. One day, driving her from work, we engaged in a conversation about our relationship. After pulling up to the sidewalk in front of her sister's house, I turned my head lights off.

The neighborhood was surprisingly quiet with only a few vehicles parked on the area. The outside lights were on, but one could barely see the outline of the dead end street. Cars as well as people passed by from time to time.

"Thank you," she said as she opened the car door. I grabbed her left hand.

"Can we talk for a second?" She turned, still holding the door opened, and stared into my eyes. "Talk about what?"

"About us. I-I . . ." I tried to speak, but my voice sounded hoarse. I cleared my throat and tried again. "I really don't see why we're separated." She closed the door.

"Clesio, there's. . ." She hesitated over the next word. She took a deep breath "There is no point in being in a relationship that isn't going to work."

"Why wouldn't it work?"

"We tried before, but it didn't work. What makes you think it'll now?"

"We aren't separated because our relationship failed. We are separated because of people's mouths." Hesitating, I placed my right hand on her left hand and slowly tightened my fingers between hers.

"Exactly, people don't want to see us together."

"Edna, it only takes two people to build a relationship, not the entire world. We shouldn't care what people say or think of us; they are just jealous. Why would we allow jealous people to destroy us?" There was a long silence. Gently, I turned her chin toward me. "Edna, all we need is love. You know, as long as we love each other, nothing else matters. Nothing."

Her eyes widened while her lips slightly stretched into a smile, but she quickly fought to hide it.

"I don't know, Clesio." She removed my hand from her chin. Her head dropped.

"What are you afraid of?" *I wish she could read my mind. It would make this situation a lot easier.*

"I don't know . . . What if we try again, and something else splits us apart?"

"We can't let that happen. Edna, as long as we trust each other, love each other, and communicate with each other, nothing, and I mean nothing, will separate us." Her lips formed a bigger smile.

She then made a straight face to hide her true feelings. *Should I hug her? Maybe not. She may get mad and push me away.* I leaned toward her, trying to read her emotions. She slowly turned toward me, anticipating my movement, but her face was still unreadable. *Damn, she's good. I can't even read her face.*

"Clesio, it's easier said than done. It's stressful to be in a relationship . . . I need to focus on school, and I can't afford to have any distractions."

I took a deep breath. "I'm not going to be a distraction, Edna. I understand you have school, work, and family, and I respect that." I turned my upper body toward her, grabbed her hand, and placed it over my chest so she could feel my heart beating. "Listen, I'm not asking you back so I can complicate your life. I'm asking you back so I can be here for you. I want to always to be here for you. I want to be the one whom you come to when you feel lonely. I want to be the one who makes your problems disappear. I want to be the one to help you with your homework—okay, fine, watch you do your homework." We laughed.

"I don't know what to say."

"Please don't say anything. Just think about it." She gently pulled her hand from my chest, and I slowly leaned on my backrest. "I better bring you upstairs before your sister comes down here," I said to break the awkward silence.

"It's okay. She knows I'm with you, and she doesn't care as long as I'm with you." She smiled.

"She trusts me." She looked at me, smiling. "Yeah, I know, I don't get it either," I joked, laughing it off.

"Thanks for everything." She opened the door.

"It's my pleasure. Tell everyone I said hi."

"I will. Have a good night."

"I can't promise anything, but I will try." I smiled.

"You are too much, Clesio. Bye now."

I waited until she entered her sister's house and drove home.

Three weeks later, we decided to give our relationship another chance. Spending time with her felt unreal. Each moment transformed into memories and looking into her eyes brought me joy. Time seemed to always fly when I was with her. She was everything I wished for, everything I wanted, and everything I needed. She was the one with whom I shared my troubles. Spending time with her felt like magic.

For two years and a half, our relationship grew stronger and stronger. When I was a freshman at Bunker Hill Community College, she was a senior at high school. We would visit universities together, searching what's right for both of us. By the time she graduated from high school, she decided to attend Bridgewater State University, which is about forty-five minutes from Boston. On her first year, I would visit her, and sometimes, I would even bring her family to visit as well.

"Surprise!" I yelled as Edna opened her dorm door.

"What are you doing here? Aren't you supposed be in school?" she asked, hugging me.

"My class got cancelled, so I decided to surprise you. I only had one class today, but my professor sent me an email yesterday, canceling it. So I immediately booked a ticket to come surprise you!"

"How do you even know I'm in my room? I could be in class." We stepped into her room and sat on the bed.

"Way ahead of you. I called your friend Hena, and she provided me with your schedule" She shook her head, impressed, with a big smile on her face.

"Oh, so that's why she has been acting suspicious. It all makes sense now. You guys are amazing."

"Besides surprising you, I came here because I want to tell something in person," I stated, hesitating.

Her eyes widened. "Oh no, what did you do?"

"Nothing this time. I just want to let you know that I got accepted into the University of New Haven in Connecticut, so now, it is official that I'm attending."

"Congratulations, I'm so happy for you." She gave me a tight hug. "Wow, I feel excited and scared at the same time."

"Scared? Why?"

"Because we are going to be over one hundred miles apart. It's hard to maintain a long-distance relationship. It's very hard to be away from you, you know. Even now that you are closer, I'm finding it very difficult to cope."

"I know it's going to be a challenge, but we are strong together."

"Maybe you are right, and we can both visit whenever possible."

"That's the spirit." She smiled and looked at her wristwatch.

"Oh crap, I'm late for class. Sorry, I have to kick you out now, unless you want to stay here until I return.

"No I can't. I have to run to work."

After I transferred to Connecticut, Edna and I realized that managing high volume of college and personal responsibilities while maintaining a long distance relationship was nearly impossible. We would spend as long as two months without seeing each other because we both were busy in school. Being apart was harder than we had anticipated. We even dedicated the song "We Belong Together" by Michelle Branch to each other, trying to cope with the distance.

Even with the song, which gave us hope sometimes, the long-distance relationship was too painful. I would miss many of her important events because I would be busy at work or doing homework.

One time, she planned a birthday party for her niece, and she wanted me to spend time with her decorating and being at the party, but because I had too many homework assignments and finals to study for, I failed to attend.

Besides missing the birthday party, I was never there for her school awards ceremonies, school events, or even when she just wanted to spend time with me. Distance diminished our love to the point where our relationship felt more natural as friends than a couple. As a result, on May 20, 2012, we decided it would be best for us just to be close friends.

CHAPTER 18

The Importance of Education

Sabel's support enabled me to pursue my dreams—so many things I wanted to accomplish. First, I wanted to prove to the world, especially my antagonists, that I would succeed, no matter what. I refused to allow people or unpleasant circumstances to determine my life. Second, I wanted to make a difference in people's lives and in the world. I lived a miserable life, so I wanted to ensure no one else had to experience the same hardship. Needless to say that education was the engine of my dreams.

Without an education, my dreams were impossible because I was invisible as a high school dropout. Many people would fail to acknowledge my presence since I didn't have a real career, a car, or a house. In fact, the only people who socialized with me were in the same situation as I was, because people who were improving their lives didn't have time to spend on the street with me. Not surprisingly, soon after my father evicted me, I learned that most of my friends were only my friends because of my values. Prior to my eviction, I was popular because whenever my friends needed to borrow a car or money, I was the most useful resources. Immediately after I couldn't provide any longer, my phone stopped ringing. Worst of all, when I called them for help during my eviction, they all justified why they couldn't help me.

Also, as a high school dropout, I wasn't doing anything productive to prove my capability. I would sleep, work, and hang out with my friends, and the cycle would be repeated. One day, standing in front of a mirror, I knew I had several questions to answer to myself. Who am I? What kind of husband and father do I want to be? What kind of son am I? How do

I want to be remembered? Even though it took me awhile to understand who I was, the answers were simple: I want to be a father, not a dad. I want to watch my future son or daughter growing up. I want to advocate for my family without government assistance. I want to have a career that will allow me to spend time with them so that when my son asks me to bring him to soccer practice, the answer will not be always no because I have to work multiple jobs in order to bring food to the table. Lastly, I want to help my mother in Cape Verde.

Thus, I enrolled in Boston Adult Technical Academy (BATA) in January 2008. When I first enrolled, I was told it would take me at least two years to satisfy their graduation requirements because I was too far behind. But because I didn't have the much time, especially after spending two unproductive years on the street, I wanted to fast forward my education as much as possible. Understating that this mission would take some serious commitments, I immediately began working as hard as I could to graduate according to my agenda.

I eliminated many recreational activities, such as watching television, going out with friends, and playing video games. I completed school assignments multiple times until I performed them to perfection. I would finish my homework and study during any available time—during my work breaks and leisure, in the car, and at home. Eager to learn, I stayed after school to meet with my professors for clarification and sometimes to talk about college. My hard soon work paid off. By the end of the school year, I had completed all my graduation requirements and graduated on June 6, 2009.

Being the first person in my family to attend college without any financial support, having been homeless at one point in my life, and not knowing how to speak English well challenged the achievement of my dreams. When I graduated from high school, I didn't know how to complete the intricate college applications and had no incentive to do so without financial resources. If it hadn't been for one phone call, I probably wouldn't ever have gone to college.

A few days past my high school graduation, and a day after explaining to Sabel my inability to enroll into college, Sandro and I were sitting at Sabel's living room. Sandro was surfing on the internet while I was watching episodes of *24*, a television show, when the home phone rang. The phone rested on the computer table, where Sandro was setting. He looked at me, and I glimpsed back at him. I was annoyed with the phone rings, interrupting my show, so I quickly resumed watching.

"Hello?" Sandro answered the phone. "I'm sorry, but I think you dialed the wrong number. No one by that name lives here." I instantly paused the television and intensely stared at him. "No . . . no . . .," he continued denying, while shaking his head. "Elisio doesn't live—"

I promptly jumped and snatched the phone from his ear. "Hello? Hello? This is Elisio."

"What the hell was that? Since when are you Elisio?" Sandro moved his lips, confused.

I placed my hand over the mouthpiece of the phone and whispered, "It's a long story. I will tell you later. Hello? Who is this?"

"My name is Danny Rivera, a success coach from Boston Private Industry Council. I'm calling you to determine if you are interested to apply for college."

"Apply for college? How did you get my information?"

"We selected your name out of a pool of two hundred students of BATA."

"Select my name from what?" I asked, confused.

"You recently graduated from Boston Adult Technical Academy, right?"

"Yes."

"That's why I'm calling. I assist students with college applications."

"How am I supposed to go to college if I can't afford it?"

"Don't worry about it now. I will help you with this process. Are you interested?"

"I'm for sure, but another thing. I lost my green card a few months ago, so I don't have any other documents to prove my alien status."

"Elisio—it's Elisio, right?" Immediately I thought back to the conversation I had with my father right before I departed from Cape Verde.

By the way, Clesio, the ink on your birth certificate was smudged and made your name look like Elisio. That's how Immigration registered you. So when you get here, people will call you Elisio.

"Yeah, it's Elisio Depina."

"Elisio, don't worry, together we can do this. If you are available to meet me right now, we can discuss your status in person and apply. I'm here at the Bunker Hill Community College. Do you know where it is?"

I could feel my hope building as he spoke. My voice became excited, and my face broke into smile. Sandro was still trying to figure out what was happening.

"Yes, I know where it's located. I'll be there in thirty minutes. How can I identify you?"

"I'm sitting in the main lobby, wearing a gray suit with a tie."

Thirty minutes later, I walked through the main entrance of BHCC and headed toward a man matching the description. My heart began pounding as though I were going to a job interview. I took a deep breath before walking in.

"Are you Danny? I'm Elisio." My voice sounded hoarse. "Excuse me." I cleared my throat. Danny stood up and shook my hand.

"Yes, I'm Danny. I'm glad to meet you," he expressed, smiling. "Was it easy getting here?"

"Yes, other than getting lost three times, it was fairly easy." We both laughed. He invited me to have a seat while he sat down.

"As you already know, my name is Danny Rivera. What I do is helping students, like yourself, not only enroll into college, but get through college."

"But what if a student doesn't have money to pay for it?" I hesitated, anticipating that he would say, "In that case, you are on your own."

"There's financial aid available for students who earn insufficient income to pay for their education."

My eyebrows rose. "Financial aid? What is financial aid?"

"Financial aid is a federal grant." My eyes widened. "It's free money."

"Do you really mean there is a possibility I might receive free money to pay for college?" I asked in disbelief.

He looked at me, his mouth stretched into a smile. "Yes, that's right." *What about that! I may have a chance to pursue my dream after all.*

"So if I'm eligible for financial aid, can I start this semester?"

"Well, we are a month away before school starts in September, so if you bring all your documents as soon as possible, you will." My head dropped. My eyes turned watery. Danny's eyebrows narrowed as if pointing at me. "You don't seem happy about starting this semester," Danny stated, confused.

"I just realized that I can't start school this semester."

"Why?"

"I lost my permanent green card, and it will take ninety days to replace," I said inaudible.

"Oh, that's not good."

"Tell me about it."

"Can you call the Immigration Center and address your situation? They may consider speeding up the process?"

"I did many times, but they don't pick up their phone." There was a moment of silence. Danny looked at me with sad eyes.

"This is what I want you to do. Go to the Immigration Center, address your issue in person, and politely ask them if they can give you a letter stating that you are waiting for a new green card. We can use the letter until you receive your green card so you don't have to delay your education."

"Oh my God, that's a good idea." My face led up into a smile. "It's still early. I'm going there right now."

"Oh, there's that smile again."

"Thank you for your help."

"No worries, I will always be here."

I rushed to the United States Citizenship and Immigration Services: Application Support Center, about a ten-minute train ride from Bunker Hill Community College. Upon arriving, I could see a long line, going zigzag. *This will be an interesting day.* After waiting in line for nearly an hour, the clerk called.

"Next!" Slowly, I approached the desk. "How may I help you?"

"Hi, my name is Elisio, and I'm trying to apply for college this semester, but I recently lost my green card. I have already applied for a replacement, but its process will take three months. That's why I'm here to see if there is any possibility to get a letter to prove that I'm a legal resident."

"Why don't you just show them your passport?" the clerk asked.

"Colleges require three forms of identification. I'm using my passport and driver's license as governmental IDs, but I still need something to prove that I'm here legally."

"I'm sorry, but I'm afraid there is nothing I can give you. You have to wait for you green card and apply for college the following semester," the clerk refused firmly.

I slightly raised my head and looked into his eyes. Then my head dropped while I slowly turned around to leave. I walked a half the length of the room and stopped. *Clesio, you cannot afford to wait any longer. You have already lost so much time.* I took a deep breath, turned around, and stood in line again. The clerk immediately glanced at me and continued to serve the two people in front of me.

"Next!" the clerk called. Hesitating, I took a couple of steps toward him.

I cleared my throat. "I'm sorry, I don't mean to bother you, but I cannot afford to wait until next semester. Please, I just need a letter, stating that I'm waiting for my new green card."

"I already told you. I don't have the authority to write you a letter."

"Is there any one I can talk to?" I insisted.

"I'm not sure if that is possible, but if you want, you can come back tomorrow and talk to the supervisor. He is gone for the day." I felt little hope building in my body.

"Thank you, thank you very much. What time do you guys open?"

"We are open Monday to Friday from 8:00 a.m. to 4:00 p.m."

"Okay, thanks. I will come back tomorrow."

That night, sleep eluded me, wondering if I would receive the letter. I, in fact, got up throughout the night to go to the bathroom and drink water. Anxiously, I started getting ready at five thirty in the morning, and by seven o'clock I arrived at the center. I patiently waited until they opened the door.

"Good morning," the same clerk greeted me, smiling.

"Good morning," I replied.

"Have a seat and wait for the supervisor. He is normally here by 8:30 a.m."

About forty minutes later, a man walked toward me. I stood up.

"Hi, are you Elisio?" he asked as he extended his hand to give me a handshake. "I am the supervisor. My understanding is that you request to see me."

"Yes."

"Come to my office." The clerk and I followed him to his office. He pulled me a chair. "Please have a seat." The clerk explained the situation. "How long has it been since you applied for the replacement?"

"A little bit over a month now."

"Did Immigration send you a confirmation letter, stating that they received your application?"

"Yes, I received it three weeks ago."

"Great! Just bring it, and I will certify it."

"Okay, I will go get it and be right back," I said as I stood up.

"Also, bring your passport and be sure you bring that one with your visa on it."

"I will. Thank you very much."

About two hours later and without having breakfast, I returned and stood in line for nearly an hour. The supervisor then certified my confirmation letter. Excited, I hurried out, looked at the letter, took a deep breath, and threw my arms up into the air. I felt a big release. *Yes, Clesio, you are going to college!*

"Hello, Danny! This is Elisio. I'm calling to give you the good news. Immigration just gave me that letter."

"Great! That's really good. Where are you now?"

"I'm close to Bunker Hill Community."

"I'm here, so if you want, come here, and we will submit your application today."

"Sure! I will be there in less than twenty minutes."

I arrived and saw Danny sitting down at the lobby near the main entrance. As I entered the main lobby, he stood up and walked toward me. I increased my pace while waving the letter up in the air.

"You the man," he said, smiling as he gave me a high five. Proudly, I nodded. "Let's get this thing done." He returned to his chair, and I followed.

"How are you?" I asked as I sat down.

"I'm fine, can't complain. How are you?"

"I'm tired and hungry. I haven't eaten anything yet." His eyebrows rose.

"It shouldn't take more than ten minutes since we've already done most of the work that other day. You still want to apply to come here, right?"

"Yes, that's right. How long does it take until they reach a decision?" I probed.

"One to two weeks."

"Oh, that's not so bad."

About seven minutes later, he looked at me, smiling. "Mr. Depina, you're all set!" he uttered, excited.

"Awesome, thank you for helping me."

Waiting for the decision was painful. A minute felt like an hour, an hour felt like a day, and a day felt like a week. I checked our mailbox three to four times per day. In fact, many times, I met the mailman halfway and walked him back to our mailbox. Nine days later, I spotted the mailman heading to our mailbox. I instantly ran downstairs.

"Is there any mail for unit C?" I asked the mailman, catching my breath.

"I can tell you are expecting an important letter," he stated while handing me all the mails for unit C.

"Yes, I'm. I'm waiting for a college decision."

"That's important. Good luck!"

"Thank you."

I quickly scanned through the envelopes and saw a letter from Bunker Hill Community College. I ran upstairs, threw the rest of the mails on the kitchen counter, and went to my room. I looked myself in the mirror and took a deep breath. *Clesio, this is it.* Shaking, I tore the envelope, ripping a little corner of the letter. I quickly glanced through where it said, "Congratulations on your acceptance. You have been accepted to the Bunker Hill Community College." I jumped up and down, singing, "I'm going to college! I'm going to college! I'm going to college!"

CHAPTER 19

Making Sacrifices

Earning a college degree is not an easy journey, especially for non-English speakers. On average, it takes non-English students three and a half years to complete an associate's degree at Bunker Hill Community College (BHCC). BHCC is a two-year institute only if one starts with college-level courses right away. But most of its students are non-English speakers; as a result, they are placed in English as a second language (ESL) courses.

I was one of those students; I was placed in the second level of ESL. I had to finish second-level and third-level ESL courses before I could move to the college level. Thus, it would take me three and a half years to earn my associate's degree. However, I didn't want to spend that much time in a community college. I wanted to graduate in two years. I developed a strategic two-year plan to map out my goals. My two-year plan indicated that the only way for me to graduate in two years was by being exempted from the ESL levels and taking six courses each semester and four courses in the summer.

I knew from the beginning that it would require more than developing a two-year plan. It would require my full commitment, patientce, dedication, and discipline. But I was confident and willing to do whatever it took, even if it meant taking the last breath in my body. After perpetually evaluating my options, I galloped to Admissions, requesting to be exempted from ESL courses. With a repugnant face, the admission personnel referred me to my professor Alexandro Massaro, who at the time also was the coordinator of the ESL Department.

"Hi, Professor Massaro," I said, catching my breath.

He was on his computer, turned to me, and removed his glasses.

"Eliiisiooo, come in," he invited me in a happy voice. "You don't look happy. What's wrong?"

I was still breathing heavily for sprinting from Admission to his office, about two minutes way. My knees were shaking uncontrollably. I took a big breath, and I collapsed in a chair opposite from his.

"Nothing. I just want to know if it is possible to skip my ESL courses. I created my two-year plan." I pulled my notes from my backpack and sidled closer. "See," I continued explaining, "If I'm exempt from ESL courses, I will graduate in exactly two years." *Please don't say no. Please don't say no.*

He raised an eyebrow, and his eyes widened. He then rolled his chair closer to me. "It's too late to skip this semester, and in order to even consider getting exempted from ESL courses, you have to demonstrate that your English is strong enough to be at the college level," he explained carefully.

"Is it possible?" I asked as he reached and placed his hand on my shoulder.

"It *is* possible but extremely difficult. Remember, you have to improve not only your speaking skill but also your witting and reading." My face started to glow. I felt tremendous relief. *I can do this.* "Have you been to the language lab?"

Now my eyebrows rose and tightened into a V. "Language lab? What's that?"

"It's a place where you can practice your English," he explained.

So for my remaining time at Bunker Hill Community College, I logged ninety hours in the language lab and thirty hours in the Tutor Center, trying to improve my English. To master my writing even farther, I worked closely with Mr. Massaro, where I would write and revise my assignments four or five times. I would write my first draft, send it to Mr. Massaro for comments or opinions, and he would resend it for a more creative revision. This cycle repeated until we both were satisfied with the end result.

Because English wasn't my first language, I faced many challenges besides academics. Since my brain wasn't familiar with the English language, it would process words or phrases at a glacial pace. Therefore, following lectures was enigmatic, requiring me to devote my full concentration; otherwise, I would be lost.

Taking notes was also problematic because by the time my brain processed and filtered important information, professors would have already a lot of essential information before I could write the first information down. In classes in which my instructors allowed me to record their lectures, I would record and then listen to them over and over until I understood the materials. But for others, I had to rely on my brain, PowerPoint, and reading in order to learn.

Reading was my biggest enemy because I was unfamiliar with half the words in most of the books. One time, my public speaking instructor assigned me to read *Language in Thought and Action* by S. I. Hayakawa and Alan R. Hayakawa. Every day, I would throw that book against the wall out of the frustration because even after I read each chapter three or four times, I still couldn't understand it. I would be mad at the authors for using too many big words. I would experience even greater frustration with my textbooks because they contained not only big words but also technical words. To conquer those textbooks, I had to read them seven to eight times despite the high volume of reading I was required to do. I was assigned eight chapters of reading each week since I was taking six courses per semester. While reading, I utilized different-colored highlighters for future reference. I used bright green for main ideas, blue for supporting ideas, pink for definitions, and bright turquoise for unfamiliar words. After the reading, I would revisit each chapter to take notes.

If reading was the enemy, writing was the general of the army. My first course in college was the first-year seminar. At the end of the class, my instructor asked me to write a half-page of autobiography. Panicking, I scratched my forehead, trying to figure out how I was going to produce what at the time seemed impossible. Writing was never my expertise, especially since I came from a country whose Creole language had no formal grammar rules to one with strict language grammar rules and a rich vocabulary.

I sat in front of my computer for nearly an hour, stumbling over words, only to write my first sentence. Too many thoughts formed in my head, but I couldn't figure out a way to transform them into writing. The more effort I exerted on the assignment, the less progress I seemed to make. What else can I write? Maybe if I drink water, I will be more productive. I lunged through Kaila as I stepped into the kitchen at Sabel's house, abruptly opened the refrigerator, and surveyed what to drink, while thinking about my writing. In my head, my ideas appeared well organized, and they read smoothly, until I attempted to write them down. After spending nearly two hours writing, unsatisfied with the result, I submitted a work with a little less content than the professor's requirement. A week later, Professor Massaro returned my paper covered with red corrections. Clearly, I had fought a battle!

When I first attended Bunker Hill Community College, I wanted to graduate within exactly two years and then search for an employment. However, the more I learned, the more I realized the need to learn more. Besides, learning wasn't all about me anymore. I wanted to make difference in people's lives, but I realized that this mission was only possible if I changed my life first. I wouldn't have the courage or confidence to motivate someone to finish his or her education if I haven't done it myself.

During my college years, I was able to practice my true passion, helping students adapt to the college environment and sharing with them goal-setting, time management, and study tips. I enjoyed seeing the smiles on other students' faces after I helped them solve their problems. I knew then that I wanted to be involved in easing students' lives. As a result, I became a new-student mentor while working to complete my associate's degree. As a mentor, I worked closely with students, guiding and encouraging them to utilize campus resources.

My involvement in people's lives motivated me even more to further my own education beyond an associate's degree. I wanted to learn communication skills so I could interact with others professionally. Also, I wanted to reinforce my value as a role model so I could confidently tell people not to give up. My hard work paid off. I graduated in exactly two years just as I planned.

After Bunker Hill Community College, I immediately enrolled as a junior at the University of New Haven. I started classes in fall 2011. I wanted to graduate within one and a half years, not a day more. Thus, I began to plan my courses and activities, identical to the one for Bunker Hill Community College. To complete all my graduation requirements according to my timetable, I had to take six courses each semester and four during the summer—a battle that I knew would require more than planning, goal setting, and time management. This battle required rigorous behavior management. But I was ready and armed for anything!

I took only five courses in my first semester to smooth the transition. After that, I registered for six courses each semester, even though I knew it was going to be a challenge. My courses included Advanced Investigative Techniques, Criminal Procedure II, Forensic Science Laboratory, Introduction to Forensic Psychology, Experimental Methods in Psychology, and Introduction to Community Psychology.

Even with my overwhelming schedule, I wanted more than just passing those courses. I wanted to maintain my 3.8 GPA. To balance my schedule and devoted more time for school, I reduced many of my recreational activities, such as watching television and playing games. I had to carefully manage my time to stay organized. Because at first I struggled to resist watching television and stick to my agenda, I developed a policy for myself.

Chapter 1, Section 1, Television Policy:

1. On the weekdays, except on holidays, I, myself shall not watch more than two hours of TV.

2. On weekends, except on school breaks, I, myself shall not watch more than four hours of TV.

Chapter 1, Section 2, Television Punishment:

1. Violation of the television policy will be punished by not watching TV the next day, requiring completion of the Red Code To-Do list, or both.

Chapter 1, Section 3, Bedtime Policy:

1. On school days only, I, myself must be in bed by no later than midnight, unless there is an emergency, or I must complete the Red Code To-Do list. If there is an emergency or a Red Code list, I, myself must be in bed as soon as possible.

Chapter 1, Section 4, Bedtime Punishment:

1. Violation of the bedtime policy will be punished by completing all Red Code assignments the next day.

Chapter 2, Section 1, Time Management Policy:

1. When any assignment is scheduled in red, I, myself must complete it on or before the specified time.
2. Record all monthly assignments on the door calendar and all daily activities on the phone.
3. Devote two hours per day assisting and socializing with other students.

Chapter 2, Section 2, Time Management Punishment:

1. Violation of the time management policy will be punished by reducing television hours to catch up with the schedule.

This strict policy enabled me to manage my school, work, family, and leisure time. With an elaborative plan, allocating more time toward school, I completed my second semester with four As and two Bs and still had time for helping, encouraging, and motivating other students who were experiencing similar challenges.

I developed several motivational PowerPoints and presented them at middle schools, high schools, and colleges all over Connecticut and

Massachusetts. Through-out all presentations, utilizing my personal story, I demonstrated to the audience how life is as wonderful as one makes it. Life is the result of our decisions. We can simply decide to give up during tough time, or we can perpetually rise up, even stronger every time we are thrown down.

Earning As and Bs was only the beginning of my success. I still had a long way to go. I was excited, but tentative about the overwhelming challenges of taking four courses over the summer, especially since school wasn't my only responsibility. Scrambling between my intensive summer classes and work left me with no time to enjoy the exquisite summer weather. Unintentionally, *sorry, no,* and *I can't* became my common responses to my friends' requests to hang out.

One day, I hastened home from work, planning to study and finish some of my homework, only to find my best friend Euclides parked outside of my aunt Sabel's home, waiting for me. Euclides, a tall thin young man in his midtwenties, wore a Boston Celtic jersey matching his short and sneakers.

"Ago," he said, trying to get my attention. "Ago, what's up?"

I turned to the familiar voice, walked toward him, and sat in his car.

"What are you doing here?"

I quickly peeked at the backseat, where he had variety of beach items, such as plastic life vests for children, little sand buckets with their shovels still attached to them, and other beach ornaments for children.

"It's hot out. Let's go to the beach."

"I'm sorry, I can't. I would love to, but I have to work on my research paper. It's due in two weeks. You know how intense summer classes are. I have to keep up because if I fall behind, it will be extremely hard to catch up," I explained, brokenhearted.

"No worries, I understand." His head dropped.

"Who else is going?"

"I'm just taking my kids."

"The kids! I hate school right now. I want to go to the beach with those adorable girls." *Clesio, go to the beach. You still have two weeks to finish this paper. Oh damn, it's red coded. Clesio, there will be a lot more opportunities to go to the beach, but if you don't do this paper, you will fail the course, and you will not graduate on time.* "Please give me two weeks, and then I'll go with you."

"Bro, you don't have to worry. We'll go next time."

His words didn't match his gestures. He concentrated his focus out of the window to hide his true emotion. He definitely wanted me to accompany him, but he understood my commitment to school, and he would support me, even if it meant going to the beach alone.

"Thanks for understanding. Let me not take more of your time. Hit me up when you return." I gave him a high five as I opened the car door. My steps felt as if someone added more weight to them. Fighting to convince the thought that it was time to study, not go to the beach, I scrambled to separate the main door key. Though I didn't turn, I could feel my friend staring at me.

While my friend was having fun at the beach, I completed my homework and studied from 5:00 p.m. to 11:00 p.m. First, I conducted all the research recorded in red and then read and analyzed two chapters—one for my abnormal psychology course and the other for sociology. This glacial process lasted all summer.

Although school reduced my fun time and was even stressful sometimes, it felt good to graduate with a 3.6 GPA in exactly one and a half years, just as I had planned. I graduated with a bachelor of science degree in criminal justice—investigative services on January 19, 2013.

But my education didn't stop with my bachelor's degree. I was too involved to stop now. Plus, I repeatedly tested my limitation and discovered that I didn't have one. My triumphs proved over and over that I was capable of accomplishing more than I can imagine. My name began spreading—some referred to me as unstoppable, while others questioned my humanity. How can an immigrant be so successful? How does he learn English so quickly when he couldn't even speak a word just a few years ago? How does he maintain a high GPA while still giving 110 percent to his other million responsibilities? Where does he get the energy?

But I didn't have the time to answer any of these questions. Instead, I allowed those questions to answer themselves.

On January 2, 2013, before attending my commencement ceremony, I started my graduate program at the University of New Haven in Connecticut, studying public administration. My graduate program introduced greater challenges than my undergraduate studies. Though the school was the same school, everything seemed to have changed, including my friends. Most of my close friends graduated with me and had either transferred to pursue their master's or started their new careers. Despite the challenges, I was destined to be successful. Okay, I was bluffing. I didn't know what I was destined to be. The only thing I knew for sure, was that I was committed to work as hard as I could to be successful—immersing myself in a new culture and pursuing a vigorous academics curriculum while still learning the language. I wasn't afraid of the demands of learning or facing other obstacles, not even for one second. In fact, the more I learned, the more curious I have become, and the more I wanted to learn.

Just as I had created my undergraduate master plan, I swiftly developed a graduate master plan. I set my goal of completion in one year, not a day more. In order to accomplish this, I would have to take four courses each trimester and two summer courses. Another enigmatic battle!

During my first trimester, I registered for four courses: Writing and Speaking for Professionals, Macroeconomics and Microeconomics, Urban and Regional Economic Development, and Public Policy Formulation and Implementation, while undertaking the writing of this book. Knowing the degree of challenge, I started to wake up at 5:00 a.m. to either write or do homework before departing for work and school. On my days off from work and the weekends, I would set my alarm clock at 6:00 a.m. to write until 9:00 a.m. and then head to school to do homework. On the days I worked, I would write from 5:00 a.m. to 7:00 a.m., work from 8:30 a.m. to 4:30 p.m., and do homework until class began at 6:00 p.m. When I got out of school at 9:00 p.m., I would run home to cook and write again until midnight. I adhered to this schedule until I successfully fulfilled my graduation requirements.

My hard work and perseverance paid off. I finished my master's degree on November 27, 2013, and moved back to Boston the following Saturday. That Saturday was mostly sunny but still cold, with highs in the mid thirties. The winds blew at five to ten miles per hour northeast, which switched toward the southeast by afternoon.

Time seemed to move glacially. It was only about 11:30 a.m., but the day felt longer. I paced back and forth in my dorm room, anxiously waiting for my uncle Tio Nelson, my father's brother, to drive from Boston to pick me up. Tio Nelson who was tall and had a round face a long ponytail, was a father figure. He loved supporting his family. When I contacted him to be a co-borrower for my student loan, he signed the contract without hesitation.

He arrived five minutes past noon.

"Hey, grad boy!" my uncle boomed as I opened my dorm's door.

"Well, technically I'm not a grad boy yet."

"When is your graduation again?" He entered the apartment.

"January 18. You're coming, right?"

"Of course, I won't miss it for anything." He smiled proudly. "Are you ready to go home?"

"Of course. I was born ready." I led him to my room, where all my belongings were packed. We began transferring them to his vehicle. "It seems just like yesterday that I moved here, and now I'm already moving out."

Standing in the middle of the room with an awed expression on his face, he scanned around the room, studying my notes on the 27 x 37-inch easel pads, posted over my walls. Without a word, he kept nodding, clearly impressed with my notes. He then grabbed a container filled with my school supplies, while I carried my suitcase and backpack.

"That's the beauty of life. We are constantly changing and growing."

"You're right, but I'm going to miss this place." I began to walk outside, and he followed.

"Look at the bright side. You're soon going to be with your mother. I'm sure that is going to be fun."

"I can't wait. That is what kept me alive during tough times."

"What? Your mother?" he asked as he opened the trunk.

"Not just my mother. But the feeling of living with her one day, you know?" I loaded my belongings into the trunk. "I've never," I continued, "lived with her before, so I'm curious to know how the love of a mother feels like."

He paused for a moment before dropping the container into the truck and awkwardly hugged me sideways.

"You're a strong young man, you know that? That's why you are so successful, and I've no doubt you're going to be successful in anything to put your mind into. You may not realize this yet, but you're one of a kind. Many people would have given up if they have gone through half the things you overcame." He slowly released me.

"Thanks, I really needed to hear that."

"You're very welcome," he said with a grin and amusement.

We resumed carrying the remaining of my possessions.

A few minutes later, while I was rearranging the trunk, trying to fit everything, my uncle handed me the last box.

"Okay, I think this is the last of it. Good thing you didn't have a lot of things." He closed the trunk and the back doors of his car.

"I should go take a last look just to make sure I got everything. I also want to say goodbye to my room. Well, my ex-room."

He smiled. I rushed inside and leaned behind the door as I gently closed it behind me. I closed my eyes. Instantly, many thoughts flooded my mind. *Wow, Clesio, you did it.* My mind quickly drifted back to where I began and walked me through from the affection of my grandmother and my mother to the miserable life of a five-year-old boy, to the constant beating of my aunts, to a depressed life with my father, and to the successful man leaning behind the door. I wasn't sure why my mind summarized my history for me. But it made me realized that hardship wasn't excuse for failure. Circumstances didn't seem to have an impact on the outcome as much as the responses or decisions have. Now I could see that it didn't matter what circumstances I was in. It was how I responded to those circumstances that really mattered. I'm only successfull today because I perpetually refused to allow circumstances to determine my life.

I returned a moment later. I ran and entered the car.

"Ready?"

"Ready," I repeated as I took a deep breath and released it slowly.

I leaned my forehead against the widow and watched my past get smaller and smaller as my uncle drove away.

CHAPTER 20

On the Brink of Success

Although finishing my education was an important achievement to me, bringing my mother to the United States was my biggest dream. I submitted a Form I-130, a petition for an alien relative, to Immigration to bring my mother to the United States during my senior year as an undergraduate. Since I am a naturalized citizen, the process took less than a year. As a result, she arrived in Boston on January 29, 2013, a week after my undergraduate commencement ceremony. My mother resided with my aunt Sabel in Boston until I finished my master's degree and found our own place to live.

Even though I traveled to Boston to be a guest speaker for Success Boston on the day she arrived, I wasn't able to see her because I had to rush back to Connecticut for my classes. In fact, due to a blizzard, work, and school, it took two months before I could reunite with her after ten years.

On March 1, 2013, I went to Boston to surprise her. Immediately after I extied the bus, about a three-minute walk from Sabel's house, my heart began palpitating. My blood vessels began throbbing, and I noticed my hands were sweaty and my knees shaking. I unconsciously kept taking deep breaths. As I approached my aunt's house, my steps felt heavier and heavier. *I wonder how she looks now.* It felt magical, but my mind was riddled with anxiety and assumption of how my mother would receive me. When I finally arrived at the door upstairs, I took a long deep breath and slowly exhaled before entered the house.

Standing at the kitchen counter, reading mails, Sabel craned her head to see who was entering the house.

"You? What are you doing here?" Sabel asked, surprised.

"Where is my mother?" I whispered, looking around.

"You just missed her. She went to Brockton with Fatima."

"Damn! Language, I know, I know. I'm sorry."

She smiled. "What, she didn't know you were coming?"

"No, I wanted to surprise her."

I lifted myself to sit on a high stool opposite her, and looking down, I placed my hands over my eyes while exhaling slowly.

"Call Luis to bring you."

"Oh my God, you're a genius."

I jumped out of the high stool, kissed her on the cheek, and dialed Luis's number.

My cousin Luis—a tall, long faced, and in his midtwenties—arrived at Sabel's forty minutes later, and we swiftly departed for Brockton and arrived at Amelia's in just a moment later. As we parked outside, I looked at Luis, and he looked back at me.

"Are you ready?" he asked, patting me on the shoulder. Slowly, I turned my head toward him, wide-eyed, and shook my head in slow motion, as my eyebrows rose. "You will be fine," he added.

"I hope so." I took a deep breath. All the parts of my body were shaking. Wringing my hands under my gray sweater, I stared at the house, watching shadows pacing back and forth. I exited the vehicle and walked toward the house. At the door, I glanced at Luis, and he nodded, signaling me to knock. I took another long deep breath and knocked. Taty, Fatima's daughter, opened it.

"Oh man, you just missed your mother. She went to church with Mama. Did you tell her you were coming?"

"No. I wanted to surprise her! I'm going through all these emotional wringer for no reason. I don't know how much more I can take."

Her eyes widened. "So you still haven't seen her yet?"

"No.I planned to see her two weeks ago, but the blizzard ruined my plan."

"Come in! Hi, Luis, how have you been? People don't see you."

"Good. I know, I've been busy with work and family."

We walked to the kitchen and sat at the dinner table. Fatima's other daughter (Amelia) was washing the dishes, while her two-year-son (Eiden) was playing with toy cars. Linklin, Fatima's husband, was in the basement, watching television.

"Clesio, there's food in the refrigerator. Please help yourself. You aren't a stranger," Amelia offered, pointing toward the refrigerator.

"Naaah, I'm too excited to eat. But, Luis, feel free to serve yourself."

I could hardly wait to see my mother. Seconds felt like minutes, minutes felt like hours, and hours felt like a day. Every minute, I could feel my body temperature raising.

"Clesio, finally you will see your mother. It has been ten years, right?" Taty asked.

"Ya, ten years."

"Wow, I can't survive without my mother. I'll go crazy if I don't see her for a week. Imagine ten years."

"I know. It's the most painful thing ever."

"How are you feeling?" she asked, getting excited.

"Goood, goood," I answered, with my eyes fixed at a wall-mounted electric fireplace, located in the living room, just a few feet away, pretending I wasn't nervous.

"She's going to be so surprised when she sees you," Amelia anticipated, sitting down at the table between Luis and me. "Clesio, I'm so proud of you. You always do something to impress me. Bringing your mother here is a big accomplishment."

"That's true. Clesio is always doing the impossible," Luis agreed, smiling while looking at me, trying to get my attention. I gave him a half smile.

He leaned and placed his hand on my shoulder. "Every time I call this guy, he's graduating. One time I called him, he said, 'I can't talk right now. I'm at my high school graduation.' Less than two years later, I called him again. He said, 'Oh, I can't talk right now because I'm at my graduation at Bunker Hill.' Just a year and a half later, I called him again. 'I can't talk right now. I'm graduating today from undergrad.' And if I call him next year, he will be graduating. This dude celebrates more graduations than his own birthday!"

Though the recognition of my triumphs meant a lot to me, my mind was too preoccupied to appreciate it. I was aware of myself biting my nails but didn't pay much attention to it. I bounced from foot to foot.

"Oh ya, I'm really proud of him," Taty admitted. "He managed to accomplish all his goals despite all the obstacles. Most kids would just give up."

"Your mother must feel very lucky to have you as her son," Amelia said as Taty nodded her agreement.

Fighting my emotion, I stood up and looked away. "I really love this home!" I said, trying to change the subject.

"Thank you!" Amelia responded proudly.

Time felt as if it was stalled. Thirty minutes felt like an eternity, making me to constantly look at my phone for the time. Luis got up, opened the refrigerator, and stood there, trying to decide.

"There are rice and chicken, fish, and, if you like, there's some lasagna on top of the stove," Taty offered.

While Luis was eating, I impatiently paced back and forth.

About an hour later, I heard a car pull up into the driveway, and my heart instantly dropped. Throughout my life, I've experienced the feelings of anguish, happiness, sadness, love, and loneliness, but this feeling was different. I've never felt anything like it, not even when I first met my mother at the airport in Cape Verde. All parts of my body were reacting at the same time. Blood rushed to my heart. My knees trembled. Goose bumps. Shins tingling. Cheeks flushed.

"I think that's them," I said, looking around for a hiding place.

"Quick, go into my room," Amelia advised, leading me to her room.

My heartbeats increased every second, so I repeatedly took deep breaths. Sitting in the bedroom, I tried to recognize my mother's voice as they descended to the basement to watch a telenovela.

"I feel a strange feeling," my mother mumbled as soon as she sat on the sofa. Everyone looked at her, fighting not to laugh. "Clesio is here, isn't he?" She smiled as if she already knew the answer.

"Clesio? No, Clesio is at school. I just spoke with him, and he isn't coming until after finals," Taty lied, wondering how my mother knew.

"I don't believe you. I think he is here. I can feel him." She got to her feet, turned on the light, and stared at everyone. She then sprinted upstairs, searching for me around the house. "I know he is here somewhere."

I could hear her steps going from the bathroom to the living room. The steps got louder and louder as she approached the room I was hiding in. I quietly hid behind the door, waited for her until she walked into the room, and hugged her from behind.

"I knew you were here! I knew it! They tried to lie to me," my mother said firmly as she turned around and squeezed me.

I could feel her crying. The squeezing got tighter and tighter, and I noticed both of us were shaking. My legs were fidgeting. Her body was trembling.

With my eyes closed, it felt as if my grandmother was wrapping her arms around my mother and me. It felt like she took us to a different world. A world with no problem. A world full of flowers and love. A world with no sound, except her soft voice, singing me a bed time story. Each second was relished until I opened my eyes to find everyone staring at us, also emotional.

"Aawww. You guys are so cute together," Amelia said as she joined the group hug.

I fought to gather my emotions. I released my mother and quickly wiped my tears.

My mother wrapped her arm around my shoulders, and we walked to the kitchen and sat by the table. I sat next to my mother.

"Oh my God, look how big you're now. You're a man now." My mother wiped her tears.

"Yeah, I'm growing up very fast. But I don't like it."

She smiled. "Finally, I get to see you. I have been patiently waiting for two months." She slid closer.

I looked into her eyes and smiled. "Welcome to the United States. How are you liking the snow?"

"Too much snow! It's too much. How are people supposed to survive this? Does it always snow this much?" She asked, wide-eyed.

"No, it hadn't snowed like this for over twenty years."

"Oh, I see. It was waiting for me before it snowed this much." We laughed.

She placed her arm behind my head and gently leaned it on her shoulder, while playing with my hair.

"Nena, you must be proud of him. He's very smart. He earned his bachelor degree last year, and he is already about to finish his master's," Amelia bragged.

"Smart is a strong word!" I responded with pride.

"Clesio, you're smart, and there's no doubt about it," she persisted.

"Okay, if you insist. I'm a genius!"

"Okay, don't force it."

"What? Too much?"

"When is the graduation?" my mother asked.

"Sometime in January, but I don't know the exact day yet. But I will let you guys know as soon as I find out."

"Please let us know in advance so we can prepare to attend," Fatima requested.

"My school only provides four tickets, so I won't be able to take all of you. But you guys are welcome to throw me a party. I'm not even asking for much. Just food, music, drinking, and girls. Is that too much to ask?"

"Yes! It is!" Taty quickly responded, nodding at me, wide-eyed.

"Taty, why do you have to ruin everything?"

"Girls? Seriously, Clesio?" my mother asked, turning to make eye contact.

"Nope. No girls. I was just kidding about that part." I avoided the eye contact. "But," I added, waving my forefinger at Amelia, Taty, and Fatima, "I'm serious about everything else."

"Clesio, we have to go because I have to go pick up my daughter from the day care," Luis interrupted soon after hanging up his phone.

"Nena, are you going to Boston with us?" I asked.

"She just got here. She can sleep over, and we will bring her tomorrow since we're going to Boston anyways," Fatima suggested.

Resisting my urge to take her with me, I understood they devoted a lot of time and energy to drive to Boston to pick her up. They missed her too. Besides, I waited ten years, I can wait one more day. Luis and I left a moment later.

Ten months later, sleep eluded me on the night before my graduation. *I slept fine on my first graduation, so I don't understand why I can't sleep on this one. Damn, this is the sixth time I have to pee.* Disappointed, I wobbled into the bathroom and glanced at the time upon returning into my bedroom. It read 5:43 a.m. *I seriously need to get some sleep.* I hopped back into my bed and covered myself with two layers of blankets.

"Clesio? Clesio?" a voice called me while tapping on my shoulder. I slowly rotated toward the voice and forced my eyes open. "Time to get up, sleepyhead," my mother said. Her lips stretched into a big smile.

"What time is it?"

"It's 8:45 a.m.," she answered before leaving the room.

I could smell toasted bread, scrambled eggs, and fresh coffee.

Stretching and yawning, I forced myself out of the bed, about ten minutes later and headed straight to the kitchen.

"Breakfast is ready." She poured coffee into my mug.

"I need to brush my teeth and take a shower first." I entered the bathroom.

"Hurry up. We're going to be late. What time is the guy coming?" she shouted through the wall.

"Danny, Nena!"

"What?"

"His name is Danny." There was a short silence. "We'll leave at 10:15 a.m."

She didn't say another word, or maybe she did and I just didn't hear, but either way, I decided to leave it alone.

After the shower, anxious to munch my breakfast, I quickly put on my black pants, blue shirt, and a striped tie with blue, gray, black, and white on it. On top of my shirt, I wore a black vest.

"Clesio, your breakfast is getting cold!" she mumbled firmly.

"Coming! I'm almost done." I rushed to the kitchen, and right before I sat down, my phone rang. "Oh now you're going to call. Bad timing!"

"Who is it? Is it the guy?"

"It's not the guy. His name is Danny. He is very important to me, so I would like it if you call him by his name. He is the reason we are having this graduation. And no, that was my father."

Without a word, she walked to her bedroom. Not knowing what to expect since my parents had been separated for more than twenty years

155

and hadn't spoken ever since. *I hope they get along. What if they start arguing about their history? What if my mother refuses to talk to him? How am I going to introduce them to Danny and my friends?*

Attempting to organize my cluttered mind, I ran downstairs and opened the door for my father. His fidgety face unraveled his anxiety. He, nevertheless, tried his best to conceal his true emotion.

"How are you, Pinocchio?" my father asked as he entered the main door of our apartment.

"You've no right to call me Pinocchio—your nose is way longer than mine."

He followed me upstairs. Dreading, my father entered the house, turning his head around, looking for my mother.

"Is your mother here?" he whispered.

"Yes, she is. She is in her room." I pointed to a room across the bathroom. We treaded into the kitchen, and he immediately grabbed half of my toast and started eating it. I shook my head in disbelief. He then tried reaching for my coffee, but I tapped the back of his hand. "Not cool. Man! Pour your own coffee."

As I turned to grab butter from the refrigerator, I noticed my mother standing just a few steps from the kitchen. I instantly swallowed. I looked at my father, and he looked back at me. Desperately trying to read her enigmatic face, I gazed into her eyes, but nothing. *What is she thinking? Is she mad? Is she is angry? I couldn't tell.*

The dark skin of my father's face turned as red as tomatoes as the room was riddled in awkward silence.

"Oh, I'm sorry. I'm being rude here. Nena, this is David, my father. And David, this Nena, my mother," I said to break the silence.

My father smiled slightly, but my mother remained expressionless. Speechless, she stepped into the kitchen and stood next to me.

"There is more coffee on top of the stove," she said with a hesitant voice.

My father paused and then dropped my toast. They looked at each other for the first time. My father then looked at me and slowly stumbled around the table toward my mother.

"Hey, how are you?" my father asked in a hoarse voice while extending his arm to greet my mother.

"I'm good. Yourself?" she answered, barely audible.

"I'm okay, just hungry," he wallowed before grabbing another piece of my toast.

"You're always hungry. There isn't a time when you are full," I interjected.

"That's not true. Remember the time at Target?"

"Yes, I remember. You complained about how you hadn't eaten all day and that you could literally eat a cow by yourself."

"Well, help yourself with some breakfast, and you guys need to hurry up because Danny will be here any minute," my mother offered firmly.

"Introductions, seriously?" my father whispered as soon as my mother went to the living room.

"You have to admit. It was pretty funny, huh?"

"No, it wasn't funny. It was embarrassing."

"Trust me. If you weren't nervous, you would have found it very funny."

"Nervous? I wasn't nervous."

"Not to put you on the spot or anything, but I could hear your heart chanting, nervous! Nervous! Nervous!"

"Okay, fine. But you know her expression can be intimidat—"

"Graduation is always my favorite thing!" I quickly changed the subject as my mother walked in, facing us, to go to the restroom.

"By the way, is Tio Nelson going?" my father asked.

"No. He called me last night. He has a family emergency."

About five minutes later, the doorbell rang.

"I think that's Danny!" my mother yelled.

"Danny is here. We got to go," I said as I finished drinking my last sip of coffee. My father followed me as I walked toward the exit. My mother waited for us at the door, and I led them outside.

"Wow. You look like a million bucks," Danny complimented me, smiling.

"I try! I try sometimes! Danny, this is my mother, Noemia, and my father, David, and this is Danny, my success coach," I introduced them.

Danny exited his car, shook their hands, and held the back door for them. I walked around and sat in the front.

"You guys should be proud of this kid," Danny said as he fastened his seat belt. "He is a superstar. From the day I met him until today, he did nothing but impressing me," he added.

My father translated Danny's remark to my mother before responding. "Oh yeah, we are very proud, and there isn't enough words to explain it." Danny nodded at me. Danny slowly drove away.

We arrived at the University of New Haven just a little past noon, after about two and half hours of driving. During the summer graduation, the lawns were planted with grass and flowers of variety colors, but for this winter graduation, they were covered with gray ice and sooty snow. The parking lots were cluttered with randomly parked vehicles since the snow covered the parking lines.

As we exited the car, graduates, some already wearing their caps and gowns, and families were walking toward the David A. Beckerman Recreation Center, where the commencement was to be held. Many of my friends congratulated and hugged me.

Proudly, I briefly gave my family a tour, highlighting my favorite places and buildings on campus.

"Wow, this school is really beautiful," my mother said, impressed.

"Yeah, this is my house. Well, it was. I'm missing it already."

After the tour, we arrived at the David A. Beckerman Recreation Center, and staff directed families to sit inside the gym, while directing graduates to check in upstairs. Soon after checking in and receiving our numbers, graduates were instructed to wait on the running track, which is located above the gym. Looking down, I saw my family talking and smiling. Also, I read our names on the PowerPoint on each side of the gym. Cameras were flashing at every corner.

A moment later, the faculty marshals led us down the stairs to our reserved seats. All graduates remained standing until the president, the brass quintet, a pipe guy, faculty, and department chairs marched across the stage and formed a straight line. The president then took the stand after the national anthem.

"Please be seated." He waited for everyone to sit before continuing with the rest of the script. "I would like to thank Sandy for the powerful national anthem. So good afternoon, graduates of class of 2014." The crowd cheered. "I am proud to have the privilege to celebrate the accomplishments of our graduates today. They have came so far; therefore, we must honor their disciplines and their commitments. Let me briefly share their stories to illustrate the passion, drive, and creativity of our students. As I share these stories, I encourage you to listen closely because this is just a sample of many more remarkable stories.

"Elisio Depina," the president read my name.

The audience went wild. Applauding. Whistling. Screaming my name.

"Elisio," he continued after the cheer wound down, "emigrated from Cape Verde to the United States ten years ago while he was a teenager and didn't know a word of English. Soon after arriving, his life took a turn. He dropped out of high school and became homeless. After overcoming many ups and downs, Elisio ultimately returned to school. In January 2013, he graduated with a bachelor's degree in criminal justice, and just a year later, he completed his master's in public administration. Elisio is the first graduate of the Boston Private Industry Council-sponsored Success Boston program and has given several motivational and inspirational presentations to middle schools, high schools, and college students."

After the president told the stories of three of us, he asked us to stand so the audience could recognize us. The audience applauded, and many of the graduates near me whispered congratulations. A few moments, later after all the remarks, they began calling names of graduates to receive the diploma.

"Elisio," the chair of public administration called a moment later.

The audience screamed once more. I carefully walked across the stage, received my diploma, and had my picture taken with president. As I was walking down the stage, people were smiling, applauding, and taking pictures. I could notice my mother eyes filled with tears. I waved at her as I returned to my seat to wait until everyone received his or her diploma.

"Graduates, you should be very proud," the president said after everyone had returned to his or her seat. "Family, faculty, and friends, all of us are very proud of you. Now, you have the knowledge and the responsibility to go change the world. And that will bring this ceremony to an end. Thank you very much for participating in this wonderful ceremony, and now please join us for the reception."

People glacially made their way out of the gym, as my family weaved through the throng toward me.

Craning my eyes toward to the sky, I threw my cap into the air, and as I watched it flying, I could see the little boy flying kites with his uncle Miquel. I could see my grandmother smiling with awe. I could see the five-year-old boy reborn. Tears immediately flooded my eyes. My mother hugged me and then my father. Now we were all crying. Danny stood right next to us, fighting not to cry.

My father reached over my head and tousled my hair. "Wow. That was amazing. You're a superstar. Even the president knows you and your story. Congratulations!"

"I'm so proud of you," my mother whispered in my ear, still hugging me.

"Thank you. That means a lot to me." *More than you can ever imagine.*

"Your grandmother would be so proud of you if she were here." She wiped her tears.

"I'm sure she is here and proud." I looked up again. *Grandmother, I really miss you and your love. But don't worry, I'm fine and I will always be, even during tough time. This graduation is just the beginning of many more new journeys and success.*

Acknowledgment

First, I would like to thank my grandmother and my mother for all the love and support and for giving me a purpose in life.

I would like to thank Alice Guido, who edited this book, providing helpful comments along the way.

Christina Tilton, who guided me throughout the making of this book, developing my story as well as characters to bring this book to life.

Dr. Steven Spignesi, whose countless support, along with his knowledge and professional connections, made this dream a reality

Stay connected with Elisio Depina:

Share your thoughts about this book at:

www.facebook.com/takeactions, or

Twitter: @elisiodepina

#unbrokenboy

If you would like to bring Elisio Depina to your organization or school for motivational speech or book signing, please contact Elisio Depina at:

E-mail: *epdepina@gmail.com*

Facebook: Elisio Depina-Motivational Speaker
or *www.facebook.com/takeactions*

Website: elisiodepina.com

Printed in the United States
By Bookmasters